MILES TO CROSS

MILES

A SPIRITUAL JOURNEY ON THE OPEN ROAD

TO

BY MIKE HOWERTON

CROSS

[RELEVANTBOOKS]
WWW.RELEVANTBOOKS.COM

Published by Relevant Books
A division of Relevant Media Group, Inc.

www.relevantbooks.com
www.relevantmediagroup.com

© 2004 by Relevant Media Group

Design: Relevant Solutions
www.relevant-solutions.com

Cover, Interior design and Illustrations by Jeremy Kennedy

Relevant Books is a registered trademark of Relevant Media Group, Inc., and is
registered in the U.S. Patent and Trademark Office.

For information or bulk orders:
RELEVANT MEDIA GROUP, INC.
POST OFFICE BOX 951127
LAKE MARY, FL 32795
407-333-7152

Library of Congress Control Number: 2004094047
International Standard Book Number: 0-9746942-3-1

04 05 06 07 9 8 7 6 5 4 3 2 1

Printed in the United States of America

To J.L.H.

My love
my partner
my soul's match
my journey mate

Thank you for giving me my brilliantly imaginative angel-girl Alex
my rollicking biting singing bear-son Caleb
my life-song of joy
and thank you for believing in me even when I fail to

Awake, butterfly. It's late,
And we've miles to go together.
Basho

TABLE OF CONTENTS

INTRODUCTION

This story involves four different wanderings spread over four different years, each one with an underpinning of a search spiritually as well.

More than anything else, I had a great time. More than anything else, I understood that I was becoming me. More than anything else, I realized that the wanderlust that claimed me was more than geographical, but was definitely of a spiritual nature. I realized that God's love is less resistible than gravity.

I wasn't a wealthy American traveler. My buddy Christopher and I worked at Alice's Restaurant on the Malibu Pier, serving coffee and warm bread to the likes of Peter Frampton for the odd tip, which inevitably made its way into the shoebox under my bed, wrapped tightly in little rolls of twenty-five one dollar bills each.

The payoff was far greater than the effort. There is no value that can appropriately be ascribed to adventure. There is no calculating "sucking the marrow" out of life. There truly is no limit ... the limits are set by ourselves, far in advance of ever really living.

I lived in Heidelberg, Germany, for a semester. The weekends were gloriously long, and afforded many Eurail jaunts to neighboring cultures.

The following summer, Toph, Dean, and I bought motorcycles, and we lived saddle sore riding through the four corners of the continental U.S.

The next year, I completed my undergraduate degree at Pepperdine's London campus, and traveled through the British Isles on the weekends, which were gloriously longer than those at Heidelberg had been. My primary mode of transport was the automobile … afforded by way of hitchhiking. *The Hitchhiker's Guide to Europe* provided special encouragement, as did a very light travel budget.

My last jaunt was a south of the border surf trek that ran the entire gamut of Central America, save Panama. The honorable Barrett T. and I made use of whatever type of transport we could muster, including light air and riverboats.

The world is full of mystery. Mystery demands a quest. So get on it. Make your own pilgrimage. For each of us, there are unique miles to cross.

"Act happy, feel happy, be happy without a reason in the world. Then you can love and do what you will."—*DAN MILLMAN*

EUROPE

JANUARY 10
Heidelberg, Germany

Life is this twisting, twirling freeform enigma, and as Kafka showed, making sense of it may be the wrong pursuit. Here I am, Gregor-style, far from my modern, superficial Californian life, in a land quiet, mysterious, and beautiful. I woke up this morning in Germany. I'm excited in a strange new way. I feel like sprinting through the cold until my cheeks ice up and my breath comes in shaggy white rags. I long to drink the mystic delirium of life deeper than any other! This place reeks of a scent that is delicious and ancient. The ivy on the stone walls lining the cobblestone streets is older than the super power called America, which until now has contained my reality. I love this place, and not just because it's different.

At night the fog rolls in, and the surrounding hills recline in a cold, white shawl. It is at this time that the serene town lights appear to be fairy lights of old, and all is quiet, save for the laughter of merry elves as they make their way toward the castle for a night of pipe and song. My brother of soul, Christopher, and I have decided to challenge each other to appreciate this time we have here with a maniacal

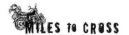

intensity. Toph (pronounced 'toe-f,' as in Chris-TOPH-er) and I roomed together last year at Pepperdine, and we had many a raucous jaunt exploring life as undergrads (including becoming two of the four founding fathers of the infamous and highly wanted by Campus Security, Lucky Lager Club. Ah, Lucky. It's more than eleven ounces of ambrosia. It's a mental challenge, as well as a laxative, situated on the inside of the twist off cap in the form of highly complex picture puzzles. I'll say no more). But our friendship has transcended itself into a challenge to live well, and to know joy, and that is the foundation of this Euro-quest. My goal is to lay down every night here and say, "This was a great day," and know that tomorrow holds joys that I've not yet dreamed possible. The greatest joy I have experienced so far is a freedom that is beyond precious.

Christopher and Jen (who have started dating since their arrival in Heidelberg last October) picked us up at the airport five days ago, and they have been showing me around this pristine town draped with crystal fog. It's so beautiful I feel like I'm in some Walt Disney dream. I said this to Toph, and he warned me, "You're awake. Don't miss a minute of this."

Heidelberg has a castle that dominates this valley, with its sandstone sprawl, a ruin, yet the most expansive, gorgeous ruin I've ever imagined. When I saw it, I started laughing. I've never seen a real castle. My suburban eyes have never seen a ruin. There's an abandoned Kmart in the town I used to live in, but that hardly counts.

Toph bought me my first dark beer. He ordered us two dunkelbeir from the Lowenbrau (pronounced *loovenbroy*) pub on the main street through the Old Town, called the Hauptstasse. It was so thick and so rich, with just a hint of sweetness, that I couldn't finish it. I asked him, "Is this great beer?" He laughed and said, "You'll think so." Then he drained my glass.

We are staying in the Moorhaus. It is an incredible four-story mansion that is situated on the hill a stone's throw away from the Heidelberg Schloss, or castle. This city has a million steps. There are ten thousand stairs leading up from the Hauptstrasse to the Moorhaus gate, thousands more leading up the walk to the front door, and hundreds more leading up to the fourth floor, which is where my room is. Our room has an incredible view of the Old Town, which is nice to look at as you try to get your breath back from climbing a gazillion stairs. Every quarter hour we hear the ganging and the clanging of the bells. Give me more of this celestial noise. I love it.

```
  no·mad
'nO-"mad, British also 'nä-
noun
1 : a member of a people who have no fixed residence
but move from place to place usually seasonally and
within a well-defined territory
2 : an individual who roams about aimlessly
- nomad adjective
- no·mad·ism /'nO-"ma-"di-z&m/ noun
```

This is going to be a good trip.

Last year I was in a relationship with a girl named Sage. Before I came here, we decided to cut it off to give each other freedom just to be for a time. I'm glad we did. This distance would be too hard to conquer. But I know she would have loved this place.

A fellow moorhaus resident named Cyndi gave me this journal. She was so nice to me when she met us at the airport; she said, "I've heard so much about you from Toph." I said, "I haven't heard anything about you," which is about as rude as I've ever been, but I wanted it so much to be funny, and instead no one laughed, and I felt a bit sick to my stomach.

JANUARY 12
En route from Vienna, Austria, to Budapest, Hungary

In Vienna I was blinded by sunlight. We are traveling as a fairly large group of Pepperdine students to Vienna for the purpose of acquiring Visas for Hungary. It is still an Eastern Block country, although

revolution is in the air. They've just last month opened the wall, so excitement and fear seem to be in the wings.

We laughed today. We played today. Toph, Dean, Dave, and I ravaged an Austrian playground and slid down the banister at the Natural History Museum. We giggled like children today as we realized that life is our plaything to enjoy. Or we may have still been feeling last night's pre-travel party. Before we headed down to the station last night, Dean lined us up on the curb and asked each one of us in turn, "Do you have your Eurail? Do you have your passport?" I was laughing so hard at his militant motherliness that I didn't realize until he came to me that I had neither. We had an uninterrupted blast, until we woke this morning and realized we had no water to drink, and mouths of cotton.

Now we sit on a train to Budapest. Steph, a friend also staying at the Moorhaus, sits next to me. We are surrounded by natives—indigenous to the area and quite welcoming—and we are silent.

Earlier, we talked of our adventures with enthusiasm; now she reads and I write. Today I toured a cathedral (the Stephansdom) of such awesome, solemn beauty that I was stunned. I was in awe. The architecture was full gothic style, with towering pinnacles and snarling gargoyles. It was so angular that it was gloomy, and I felt that a few minor changes would have transformed it from an edifice of love into something sinister. Nevertheless, I was impressed.

Last week I did something horrible. I was an ugly American. Several of my Moorhaus friends were trying to communicate with a salesperson down on the Hauptstrasse, and getting increasingly frustrated with their limited German and the clerk's inability to translate their desires into reality. I jumped in with a totally inappropriate, "Das Fenster ist blau," which may or may not mean "the window is blue," but it offended everyone involved. The clerk walked away in disgust. My friends exited the store heated from embarrassment and frustration. I'm pretty sure I've never felt shame quite like that. I apologized profusely, as they say, but the thing was still too fresh. So as my friends walked, I dropped back, and instead of making the long trek up to our house, I walked slowly back toward our classrooms, past the university, past the pretzel vender, and then over to the bank of the Neckar. It was cold and gray, and I'm pretty sure it was a new type of loneliness that confronted me. It was the loneliness of a tremulous acceptance, of me jeopardizing my friendships before they begin. Insecurity sucks.

---

per·e·gri·nate
`per-&-gr&-"nAt
verb
intransitive senses: to travel especially on foot :
WALK
transitive senses : to walk or travel over :
TRAVERSE
- per·e·gri·na·tion /"per-&-gr&-'nA-sh&n/ *noun*

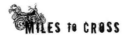

It's been four days, and I'm still not exactly past it. Confidence shaken is a wonderfully humbling experience.

JANUARY 14
En route from Bern, Switzerland, to Heidelberg

For my first travel jaunt, I am pleased. Budapest was spectacular; a dreary gray diesel film covered the cityscape like a fine dusting of volcanic ash. It was the gentle fallout of oppression imploded. Dean, Laura (Laura is also from Pepperdine), and I split off from the group and hit the magnificent Gellert Turkish Baths—it was fun to be swimming in warm, crowded, indoor pools as the only visitors not wearing speedos (I'd like to make that clear). Then we feasted like kings at the first McDonald's in Hungary—a Big Mac was like forty cents—and lovely Hungarian maidens (and a couple who could have shot-putted me) flirted with us. We decided to leave, and happened to meet up with Christopher, Jen, and Becky, who had been traveling separately due to some entrance visa trouble. To relieve ourselves of nearly useless Hungarian currency, we loaded up on food and wine. We drank. We talked. We laughed. Becky became sick. We became sober.

---

pil·grim·age
'pil-gr&-mij
noun
1 : a journey of a <u>pilgrim</u>; *especially* :
one to a shrine or a sacred place
2 : the course of life on earth

In Vienna, Toph and Jen lead Becky toward Heidelberg. Dean, Laura, and I stayed up all night talking as we lay in our second class train car. We lay on our backs and spoke of what we'd seen in a former

Eastern Block country. We spoke of what we felt were answers to the world's ills. We spoke of the dreams that we held tightly to our hearts. Laura wants to pursue law ... Dean is thinking of medicine, maybe the Peace Corps. I'm of course not sure. I want to think. I want to feel. I want to write, but certainly my brain is a tad too feeble to produce tomes of worth. I'd desperately like to have an original thought. I'm working on a philosophy of Appreciation ... which I admit doesn't have much substance, but it does have potential. The central idea is that God (in the Aristotelian sense ... the show starter, the unmoved mover) has given us, for whatever reason, life. Our appreciation of this gift is the appropriate form of worship. For example, you receive a gift from your father. A very nice gift. Let's say, (I say to Laura and Dean) you wake up on Christmas morning, and you go outside to grab the newspaper (I have no idea if they even deliver the paper on Christmas—do they? I ask, and neither Dean nor Laura know. They must, we conclude, certainly, we assure ourselves. But secretly we suspect they write it early and then go home to usher in the only hushed day in our frenetic calendar year), and as you bend down to pick up the paper, you notice that parked in your driveway is a brand new convertible Jaguar. Your dad stands behind you, and he says with

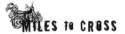

a very cheery grin (this IS Christmas, after all) that the car is yours. I think there is a key question to ask in this situation, and the question may get at some of the angst we feel ... How do you respond to your dad in an appropriate way? In other words, given this situation, what is the good life? The appreciation theory purports that the good life has at least two tenants: to be thankful, and drive the car. Yes, you could ding it, or get a ticket, or any number of less than ideal outcomes might happen. But relax! It's Christmas! Enjoy the gift, and use it well! Perhaps this is as close to praise as a lost humanity can get.

It's not much, but as I tried it out on Dean and Laura, they were kind enough to pretend they liked it.

When we looked out into the morning, we found ourselves in Switzerland ... quite easily the most beautiful place I've yet seen. Old town Bern, the capital, was quaint and picturesque. There were bears. It was quiet and happy on a bright Sunday morning, and we became quiet and happy as well. As I walked the streets of the old town, my soul was fed. We had cappuccino together. It looks like I'm learning to drink coffee. That is a beautiful thing. I admit that any beverage would taste good with the amount of cream and sugar I add, but the point is that coffee is just simply wonderful. It feels so good, warming as it goes down, warming my hands as I hold the cup, warming my excitement for the next thing, whatever it is.

Now we return. The others read. We are tired, but a smile rests on all our lips. As for me, images of what I've seen flash through my mind. As our train had rolled toward the dawn, I saw two horseback riders on a lonely hill in the morning frost, motionless, save for a twitch of tail and sweet horse-breath exhaled visibly. We marveled at the thin skeletons of trees, thickened with white and sparkling in the sunlight. I desperately wanted to free the bored, motionless bear sunk in an old-town Bernese pit. I've breathed the air of museums and cathedrals, thick with dust and time. I've seen a few more flying buttresses; I've cringed at exposed acres of jiggling pale flesh in Speedos; I've seen in the eyes of shopkeepers oppression and hope, dancing. Mountains, oh my God. Mountains like pillars holding up the sky. Life. I take a deep breath, and life fills my lungs; I rise.

Kafka can bite me. I've got to try to make sense of this thing. The meaning of life must revolve around living with love and balance. It must revolve around seeing the beauty that is found dripping from the most mundane of objects. It must revolve around making peace with yourself. It must. This might be a Zen thing, but it's also Christ, it's also Ecclesiastes. I just pray to the Holy Other that I get to keep my heart.

In the meantime, I'll worship through appreciation.

How I wish I had my camera.

JANUARY 17
Heidelberg, a typical day

When we wake up in the morning, it is still pitch black out. I sleep under the warmest down dekka, and getting out of bed is the greatest victory of my day. I don't want to. Ever. When the alarm goes off in the blackness, I moan softly. Early morning agony must be quiet. We shower down the hall and dress in silence, respectful of each other's pain.

When we walk downstairs to breakfast in the cold gray morning, we are greeted by the sad, soft tunes of the Indigo Girls. It's the album that is just called *Indigo Girls*. It is comforting to hear them day after day. I am comforted by them. We have a comfortable relationship, as in,

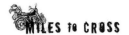

"Good morning, girls of Indigo. I'm not awake yet, but when I am, I promise to appreciate your music." Plus, they have a lyric that says, *The less I seek my source for some definitive, the closer I am to fine,* which makes sense to me at this stage of the game.

Our breakfast rolls and breads are brought fresh every morning. If there is a heaven, there will be fresh rolls delivered daily. Lately I've been settling into a routine of a warm croissant with a thin slice of cheese melted on it, Muselix stirred into my yogurt, and cappuccino that is brewed daily by either Toph or Cyndi. They host breakfast as a part of some work/study deal that allows them some travel cash. They do a fine job.

I walk out of the front door happy and warm, but by the time I reach the Moorhaus gate, my eyeballs have frozen solid.

---

vag·a·bond
`'va-g&-"bänd`
adjective
1 : moving from place to place without a fixed home : **WANDERING**
2 **a** : of, relating to, or characteristic of a wanderer **b** : leading an unsettled, irresponsible, or disreputable life

---

JANUARY 25
Heidelberg

A child went forth, so the master wrote, and what he saw he became. I would be happy to become the city of love that I experienced last weekend. Florence has warmed me, and wooed me, and I am caught. It's difficult to describe what it is that I'm in love with ... friends, adventure, life ... but I am in, deep in. On Friday, Cyndi and I wandered around the fair city and let the sun warm our bodies, which refreshed our souls. Italians here have a style that is outpaced only by their attitudes.

Inside the Duomo, swords of light from high windows pierced the darkness, vividly illuminating the dust that swirled as someone walked through and startling me with their sudden appearance; and just as suddenly they were gone, engulfed in the blackness.

We visited the Boboli Gardens and picnicked on wine, crackers, tomatoes, and cheese. After our meal, I laid back on a grassy slope and closed my eyes, enjoying the powerful sunlight casting light shadows through my eyelids, and realized I was completely happy. This is what I meant by love—I was invaded by it. Even as the bright afternoon sun flooded through eyelids closed tight, love seeped in regardless of my efforts to protect myself.

I think I may be crazy about Cyndi. Or it might be more accurate to say that she drives me crazy. It is very hard to describe. I think the life that is within her is larger than me. She is strong and creative and strange in many wonderful ways. But practically, as in a day-to-day thing, I don't think I can keep up. It appears I'm a relational asthmatic.

Today we depart for France. This adventure continues, young Mike. Don't slow. Don't tire. Simply live, and smile.

By the way, I'm beginning to be moved by art. I would have never guessed this about myself, but I am. After studying the masters of the Renaissance in our art history class, Florence was a great place to come. The Duomo, Michelangelo's David, his unfinished slaves, Donatello's David ... incredible. Jen and I scoured the Uffizi and found it is filled with wonders. The gardens there are an art form as well. I'm not sure exactly what caused it, but there were tears in my eyes more than once as I journeyed, and this is new phenomenon. It was frightening, in a way. But if this is fright, bring me some more.

JANUARY 27
Heidelberg

Venice rises immediately and inexplicably from the waters. Becky and Jen and I had a top tier adventure there. We visited the beach to splash pale feet in the water and collect shells. We laughed a ton. We laughed as funny Italian waiters tripped over themselves in an effort to serve Jen and Beck. We laughed as these two petit women hid giant beer steins in their clothing for posterity. (I'm not kidding. These tiny ladies must have been carrying twenty pounds of glassware each, the dirty thieves.) We laughed as I tried, emboldened by the night's exploits, to break down the door to our room that was so small and so cheap and so locked. We laughed, we loved, we dreamed, we learned, we lived. We found that we are very compatible travel companions, and that Italian men are very aggressive. We found that the future holds limits, but only those set by ourselves. We found a common love of life as an adventure.

When we returned, we found that Toph (or, to use his alter-ego, Tink) had been having some adventures of his own. Note to self: Have

The sea scent is moist in the air
damp with dew and
the cry of gulls.
The waves pound methodical
Consistant
roaring with a gentle thunder
rocks clattering as the sea pulls them
into itself:
first, pounded and pressed by a
great weight crashing
then, covered, surrounded,
Full of disorientation
(and a hint of smallness)
Finally, drawn irresistable
with lover's embrace
into a silent surrendering
part of the thing itself
hearing the clatter of others
as they are
met
embraced
drawn

him housebroken before we get an apartment. He isn't traveling with us at present due to a lapsed Eurail pass, and I guess to pass the time, he decided to mark a bit of the Moorhaus as his own.

I think it really shocked the person who was in the bed he selected to scent. The first time this happened was after our twenty-fifth Lucky Nite, which included a Lucky Extension (we gathered in Paul and Haney's room to watch *The Wall*, by Floyd, of course). Poor Haney was sitting relaxed in his bed as the tunes wafted gently by, and all of a sudden, through the incense and candle flame, Tink struck, laughing this silly guffaw as his relief became Haney's horror. Oh sweet joy. Some tales of debauchery are really too poetic not to share.

My guess is that this recent episode came after a long night of sampling Germany's finest. Fortunately, friends dwell not under law, but grace.

FEBRUARY 9
En route to Nice

Traveling to Nice is easier said than done. We planned to hit Nice after catching our connection in Milan—we missed Milan. Then we planned to hit Nice after catching our connection in Volgero—we missed Volgero. Now we plan to hit Nice after catching our connection in Cuneo—but I make no promises. The countryside is beautiful. I can't wait to explore and wander and discover later this summer. I'm thanking the Creative Mystery who came up with all this beauty. It is easy to appreciate when beauty beats against your senses. Jen, Beck, and I are so mellow, we will be happy wherever we end up this weekend, but we would like to end up in Nice. Now, I sit here on this train, practicing Spanish in my mind. I'm not sure why. Maybe I thought it would be nice to review what little I can remember (I've cheated my way through far too many Spanish classes to forget it all now) in light of the blitz of German homework with which our professor attacked us.

Last night on our overnight train, we met a beautiful eighteen-year-old model named Brit. We talked (the three ladies and I) until Jen and Beck fell asleep next to me on one side. Brit and I talked long into the night. She told me of her life as a model, where her travels have taken her, how many languages she speaks. I told her of my life as well. We began to talk of dreams and hopes and fears, and she seemed respectfully attentive to my Appreciation philosophy, and my book idea (which follows a dying man's journey as he finds the woman he has always loved, tells her of his love, and then rides off into the sunrise, Grecian Urn style. I don't have much dialogue mentally written. I do know he's tragically young and very healthy, except for this little fatal disease thing. He's a brilliant biological engineer, ruggedly handsome, and an internationally known Kenpo Karate competitor. And I have this doomed lover driving a Harley Davidson Springer Softtail Heritage Edition, and the final scene pans his highway ride to glory in a camera shot that starts covering the road going seventy, slowly rising to the crimson dawn, all to Lou Reed's song "Sweet Jane," sung by the Cowboy Junkies. This is important).

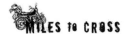

Brit fell asleep on my arm. I laid awake a long time staring at the ceiling of our train car and wondered why my heart was pounding like it wanted out. It pounds still as I write. No wonder people love Europe.

I must be buzzing on that last cappuccino.

"The best laid plans of mice and men, gang oft awry."
—ROBERT BURNS

FEBRUARY 10
En route to Heidelberg from Nice

We made it to Nice, that Jewel of the Riviera, and it was a triumphant venture. We stayed at a great hotel, had a Vietnamese meal that incited intestinal gas, and enjoyed ourselves thoroughly. Today we strolled along a sunlit boulevard and drank in the deep, blue sea. We explored a fortress that came equipped with a spectacular view, an incredible waterfall, and a mediocre burger stand. Last night we sat on the beach and gazed at the fullest moon I had ever seen in a sky so blue it ached like hunger.

The city was good, but comparable to an imitation diamond— pretty, and lacking authenticity. The things that feed the soul are found in nature.

I can't get some scenes out of my head: Brit, listening to my story as if it spoke of something transcendent, Torino and gelato and sunshine, talking late into the night with Jen and Beck, seagulls hovering and swirling en masse, crying in a dance that was precisely magical, and a great night's sleep. The fresh breeze, the sunshine bursting through the clouds to midmorning glory, the deep blue of the sea and sky, trees, waterfalls, freedom to travel geographically if not philosophically, and peace. I don't know where the peace comes from, but there are moments and even hours that it visits. If only I could get it to stay.

Thankfulness pervades.

Last week several of us from the Moorhaus had a picnic. This was high on the hill that overlooks the Neckar Valley, along a lane called the Philosophers Way (the Philosophenweg). You can see our house from here, as well as the Schloss and the Old Town. I can't believe how beautiful it is here. As prone as I am to exaggeration, there can be no exaggerating the bombardment of sense with which the flowers and valley and river and Old Town and Schloss relentlessly assaulted. We brought wine, bread, cheese, and apples, and shared a feast. Dave, Toph, and I balanced on a fence, and attempted to see who could pull or push the other off first. It was totally childish, dangerous, and fun, like something out of *Dharma Bums*. Kerouac would have been proud, and when it comes down to it, it's hard to ask for more than that.

> **vag·a·bond·ish** /-"bän-dish/ *adjective*
> *noun*
> : one leading a vagabond life;
> especially : **TRAMP**

FEBRUARY 16
Heidelberg

Last weekend our house went on a Christian retreat. It was interesting, and not totally a drag. But it didn't hit me where I am spiritually. Everyone is super-fundamental: conservative beyond description, and I dialogued very little because I felt outnumbered. I do think that there was some great time of affirmations ... we spent some time sitting in a circle and saying nice things about one another. That was nice. I joined in, because I want to be nice as well. So most of what I said was nice. But I meant what I said to Toph ... that if I could make my life like anyone's, I would want to make mine like his. There is something attractive about his life that is difficult to put my finger on, like fresh air to the fainting. Whatever it is, I want it.

FEBRUARY 22
Heidelberg

Toph and I camped out in Middle Earth last weekend. If not Middle Earth, then someplace so steeped in romance that I was beside myself in wonder.

We had seen some good country previously, on the way back from the retreat, and decided that we wanted to grab some time in those hills. So after class on Thursday, we headed down to the train station, stopping in the groceri long enough to fill our sacks with yogurt, bread, cheese, and beer. Then we trekked upwards and onwards, into the forested hills, and spent the night making Tolkien proud, elvish in our friendship, and our love of nature. When I woke up, it was early, and I walked to the edge of the forest. It opened up on a long, smooth, fertile valley, and with the sun glistening on the dew, the place was marinated in Wordsworth-esque romance. I was beside myself. I wanted to fly, to run, to open myself up to that beauty and take it all in, swallow it whole, to burst wide with beauty dribbling out the cracks … I literally did not know what to do with my early morning emotional response. So I walked back to our camp, packed it up with Toph, and started the wander back to Heidelberg. Each step left awe further behind.

FEBRUARY 28
Heidelberg

It's been a couple weeks since my last entry, and the thoughts rush through my head with no regard to my needing to make them behave. I was moved and destroyed by our East German trip. Toph and I walked on the Berlin Wall in front of the Brandenburg Gate, and watched the sun set over a free Europe. I've been detained and searched by East German guards who foresee inevitable unemployment as the iron curtain falls. My soul was shattered as I walked in and out of the concentration camp of Buchenwald (I can never forget you—Ich kann dich nicht vergessen). The nature of man at once appalls and fascinates me; the potential for both good and evil are beyond estimation.

On this trip, Steph and I have been flirting. As we walked through palaces and parkways, we hooked pinky fingers, and walked together with what a casual observer might call "idiot grins." The whole time I'm thinking "Prufrock" ... Do I dare disturb the universe? Do I dare to eat a peach? So far, the answer is no. Have I mentioned insecurity sucks?

Yet, at the moment, these thoughts are not real to me—I write them simply for the sake of memory. What weighs on me is a question asked me by my brother Christopher.

Who is the real Mike? I think he asked in response to a rearing of my pride, or my anger, or my judgment. Perhaps he sees a bit of my jealousy at his easy friendships with all. I don't know what prompted it, but I was frightened at my inability to answer it.

When no one is looking, who am I? The question scares me.

I am the master of many roles ... and each role is determined by my surroundings. I wear masks that change as the scenes around me change. But doesn't that mean there is a core, a real person that is me who is able to don the variety of masks? Wouldn't that make sense?

I hope so.

But if there is, we haven't spent much time together.

My spirit has been down lately, and I hurt Laura's feelings. This irritates me about myself, but recognizing this and changing it are two very different breeds of dog. I said to Curt (another friend who puts up with my musings) that life is a process of attempting to postpone boredom. He argued with me, and I believed everything he threw at me, but when I said it, I felt like it was truth, which means that I'm also feeling depressed and alone.

Tomorrow morning I leave for Paris.

Am I alone because I'm a jerk?

Or am I a jerk because I'm alone?

Am I afraid to be myself?

Do I even know who that is?

authenticity
is such a road
like the poem says:
   overgrown with grass
blades sharp as knives.
   skirting the surface
   is much easier
   gliding
   flying along
waving as we pass
   keeping at safe distances
friends, or those who could be,
   for safety's sake.
   safe as a tomb.
   safe as confinement
      solitaire
   safe as a ghost town
      dust dry parched
      and cracking

MARCH 28
Heidelberg

This last month flew by in a flurry of school, activity, and travel. I went to Paris with Barry and Becky (where I lost myself in the Musee d'Orsay, and got lost in the Louvre); then I went to Amsterdam with Toph.

That city is amazing—the Red Light District makes Sodom look like a nice retirement community. However, even the ugliest reality contains the seeds of the indescribably beautiful. Only how to embrace potential ...? No answers here.

The first night we were there, Toph and I bunked down at Bob's Hostel, which I suppose is a bit famous, at least judging by the number of travelers there and the amount of smoke yellowing the walls. In the morning we went to Anne Frank's house, and to a Heineken Brewery tour, where we met some cool Aussies who kept shouting, "Give that kid a dingo!" whenever someone said something stupid. It was, how shall I say? a good time. Later in the afternoon, Toph and I discovered a very inexpensive case of brown-bottle Grolsch, which proved itself delicious again and again. We sat on a bridge over a canal, consuming our find, and were people watching when we met our Australian friends from the brewery again. It was at this point I began to damage myself. Australians are merciless, and refuse to drink alone. Finally, we wandered back into Bob's bleary and late, and nobody was there. Not a soul. All of the bunks were disassembled, and the lockers were empty. It was like a scene out of *The Twilight Zone*. Not knowing what else to do (and not really caring), we found some mattresses and went to sleep in the cavernous tomb of a dead hostel. Sometime during the night, the owner (apparently) came in to yell at us to move (I'm guessing), but the noises we made were so inarticulate that I think he opted not to move us (which would have required a fireman's carry) and let us stay.

Last weekend we went to the Loire Valley as a group, and I decided that group travel is difficult. We saw three Chateaux in the Loire Valley and stayed two nights in Paris. On Friday several of us sat on the steps of Monmartre laughing, drinking red wine and singing (songs like "Alice's Restaurant" and "American Pie") with some musical hippies

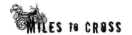

who were settled down comfortably in the '60s.

In a week this semester will end, and that just isn't possible. Yesterday it seems I was a frightened child fleeing the wrath of my parents, and now I can navigate and survive anywhere (within reason and with a little cash) ... bold, undaunted. I've grown these last few months.

There is a strange sentiment rolling within me as I think that these may be my last days in Heidelberg ever. My last days to lounge in the sun on the banks of the Neckar. My last days to stroll along the Philosophers Way in bloom. To read great literature in the outdoor cafés of Holy Ghost plaza or to laugh with friends over an export in Henniger Pub. To gaze in silent wonder at the ancient Schloss or inhale the cool spring air of this Eden-like valley. I love Heidelberg. I love Europe. I love the way life happens here. I love life, period. It is, as they say, all good.

---

wan·der
'wän-d&r
verb
1 a : to move about without a fixed course, aim, or goal **b :** to go idly about : **RAMBLE**
2 : to follow a winding course : **MEANDER**
3 a : to go astray (as from a course) : **STRAY**
b : to go astray morally : **ERR c :** to lose normal mental contact : stray in thought
transitive senses : to roam over

MARCH 31
Written at the Heidelberg Schloss

I wanted to say that huete (today) was easily one of the most beautifully fresh, sunny, green spring days I have ever seen, and as I wandered about the town and the castle, my heart leapt up and ran on the lawn through the flowers singing, and it was all I could do to keep up with it. I read the masters of literature for a while in the sunroom of the Café Journal, and then I lay down in the Schloss meadow and let the sunlight filter down through the leaves and onto my closed eyelids. When joy courses this thickly through your veins, it is hard to know how to proceed. I'm winging it. I'm alone, of course. Winging it is easy to do.

the sun rose this morning
calm, majestic
embracing clouds with the dawn
the skyscape blushing crimson,
gold,
brilliant,
gray to glory,
routine.
The moon last night was full
brooding, quiet
hiding behind tufts and wisps
of a dream
surreal it was,
and my heart pounded with me
as I moved slow
languid
swimming through the thick
muted paleness of the
half-light

The candlelight through the vase is shattered,
    Refracted,
thrust in hues of blue (of all things)
    in myriad directions
        — dancing
        — leaping
        — laughing
surrounded by wonders:
    LIFE,
        Beauty,
and me, mostly asleep.

APRIL 24
Oxford, England

Right now I'm sitting on an Oxford lawn, staring at one of the highest educational facilities in existence, and it is beautiful. Last night Dave and I slept in a small forest in a suburb of London, and today we saw the castle of Windsor (we missed the widow, so handsomely spoken of by Kipling), then hitched the seventy or so miles to Oxford. We bought some chalk, and a slate to write the name of the town we were hoping to hit, and got a couple of rides without much wait. The countryside is beauty ... it's the Shire I've imagined since I read *The Hobbit* when I was a child. Tonight we are planning on sleeping in a forested nook of the world behind a boathouse on the river. I'd love to have a fire and a satyr or two for merriment's sake.

Dave is a friend from Heidelberg who, besides being available to travel, astounds me with his coolness and flexibility (however, he does iron his polo shirts). He eagerly scours his *Let's Go*, which means our steps are directed, and I'm fine with his leadership. My only complaint is that I'm trying to stretch my money ... I'm wondering how thin it can go.

It's been two days since I left my family at the Frankfurt Lufthagen. (Two Oxford men just passed in their white tennis clothes, and one was saying to the other, "It was Andrew, you t--head," and then glimpsed me sitting there and apologized, "Sorry, old man.")

My family came to visit, and we had a great two weeks touring southern Germany and Bavaria. They met me on the last day of my finals, and we rented a car to tour together. Things went well—surprisingly well, considering the tension we've been known to muster. We drove the Romantic Road, saw Salzburg and Meersburg and Neuschwanstein, with me using Deutch as our sole form of communication to the world at large. Apparently I learned something this semester.

This world is awesome. My soul sings at every glimpse I get of this

glorious gift called life. I am noticing that I'm thinking of God more in terms of a Creator who still plays a role in things, than a totally impersonal one. Maybe that is a side effect of the "Appreciation" philosophy.

MAY 1
Tongue, Scotland

I hardly know where to begin. Each day has been so incredible. Each new place offers so much adventure, it is impossible to describe the beauty and excitement and joy I feel. Now Dave and I are witnessing a scarlet sunrise over the Northern tip of Scotland, and I am filled with awe. It isn't even 3 a.m. yet, and the dawn is here. We watched the sun set at just before midnight last night ... I have never seen such a vivid display of vibrant blue and dying gold. We are staying in the town of Tongue, in a bed & breakfast. There are islands lying quiet in the blue sea; lambs are bleating contentedly in this sparkling glen. This little corner of the globe is largely untouched by human hands, and nature here sings harmonious unhindered praises to the Mystery. I smile and watch the slow waves break softly on the beach.

We have seen a ton since Oxford. We've seen the Roman Baths in Bath, Shakespeare's birthplace Stratford, saw Banbury (we've been Banburying), and stayed alone at a great lady's house in Coventry. I'm amazed she let us stay there alone. She picked us up, gave us a hefty ride along our road, and was captivated by our journey. So she gave us the keys to her flat and told us to help ourselves to any of the food she had in the place. We made spaghetti. It was deliciously free.

We've been through Leeds to York (where there is a great cathedral) and then up to Edinburgh. (Incredible city, incredible castle, and I can't believe that's all I have to say about Edinburgh. That city is amazing, and The Princes Street Gardens beneath the castle is a Wonderland. What cracks me up is that our ride up to Edinburgh was with a construction worker, and Dave couldn't understand a word he said. Dave kept asking, "Say that again? I'm sorry, one more time? Could you repeat that?" until our driver cursed under his breath and drove in a silent smolder the rest of the way. When he got out, Dave turned to me and said, "Your turn in front.")

Yesterday, we were trying to hitch a ride to Inverness, but the man who picked us up felt we must see the North, so he got us a free bed & breakfast, bought us a meal and pints last night, and provided us with scenery that will remain etched in my imagination forever. Days like today not only prove the existence of a Creator, they prove a Creator's love of the piercingly beautiful. A thousand pardons, but this day is so fresh and new, I must excuse myself to enjoy.

Later, same day: We are camped by the shores of Loch Ness. Earlier today, I jumped into its icy darkness, only to jump out again almost immediately. I suppose legend is perfectly harmless. But as the inky waters closed over my head, that smallest fraction of thought I had as

to the authenticity of Nessie grew to horrific proportions. I clamored out like a frightened schoolgirl, and was pretty sure I saw a huge movement of water under me. (I wish. That would have been an appropriate ending to this little near-legend encounter.)

MAY 17
Santorini, Greece

I no longer believe in the word "coincidence." I know that powers much higher are in control of my life and trying (succeeding rather) at making me one of the happiest and most awe-struck people in existence.

Dave and I toured Ireland, lovely leprechaun infested Ireland, with Greece on our minds and Toph and Jen on our hearts. At the semester end, we had planned on meeting them in Greece after six weeks or so of travel.

We slept in a doorway in Galway, bitter cold and cramped, praying to the God of the homeless that the door wouldn't open to screams and a beating. And this was after an all day festival in which we made friends with lovely drunken Irish maidens, one of whom kept saying in a delightful brogue (delightful even with the slurring), "I like GALway. It is my favorite place, GALway is." I made a friend in Galway, a nine-year-old boy named Pat. I was walking out to the rock jetty to jump into the icy Atlantic. He was walking there too. As we walked, we talked about his life, his family, what he loved about Ireland (which was everything). When we got to the jumping off place, we began to strip down to our shorts, and he bent over to untie his shoes. I was watching as he examined the knot his laces had become. He attempted for a moment to loosen the knot, and then, being frustrated, he grabbed one shoestring in each hand, and pulled with as much strength as his little nine-year-old frame could muster. The knot cinched down hard; it went from being a manageable problem into an inextricable solid. Recognizing he was stuck, he looked at the knot one more time, and then looked up at me. "Are ya any good with knots?" he asked cheerfully. I was witnessing a parable. We screw ourselves to the place where we can't budge an inch, and then we look hopefully around for someone who is good with knots.

No wonder pop gurus are in demand.

We got thrown out of a meadow in Killarney, and hiked into the twilight looking for a place to bed outdoors. We ended up in a still, more out of the way lawn, under a crescent moon, with a blanket of fog lying a foot off of the ground. That place was the most magical place I've ever been. As we slept, I could have sworn I heard the tiny patter of little leprechaun boots on the soft turf.

We visited the Guinness brewery in Dublin, and stayed in the taproom as long as they would let us. Nothing could be finer. After drinking our lunch there, we walked back toward our hostel but became incurably sleepy en route. Thankfully, there was a cathedral lawn well kept and sun-drenched that invited us to nap like beggars— or kings—it's hard to say which. Later, we cruised the university looking for U2, but no luck.

But Greece was beginning to invade all waking thought. We were totally starved for some good music (Toph always traveled with a great tune archive) and some variety of friendship (I'm not saying we were sick of each other, but we were sick of each other). Plus, we NEEDED some sun. Our pale clammy skin reminded us often of our immanent mortality.

We took a ferry out of Rosslare, Ireland, and embarked on a hell trip to Athens that lasted seven days. In Athens we almost brawled seriously with a drunken hostel owner, but instead I waited until he was asleep, then sneaked upstairs and stole his shoes. They didn't fit me, but I was more interested in reallocation than ownership.

Finally we made it to the American Express office to get the message from Jen and Toph as to their whereabouts. This was the plan, anyway. There should have been directions on how to find them. There weren't.

There was no message, at least none addressed to us. (Aside: It turns out that so many fellow Pepperdine students were traveling that way, they decided to post a Pepperdine Students Message, but we knew none of this.) Dave and I felt like bawling, cashing it in, and calling it quits—we almost hopped a plane home, but instead we took the nearest ferry to whichever island it was heading to.

We made it to Santorini (barely ... if two French girls had been a bit friendlier, who knows where we would have ended up. "Mie-Kal," one of them said gently, like she was tasting a piece of chocolate, "eet ees a beautiful name," and my heart stopped. But our dialogue went only a very little further).

Santorini is beautiful, and Dave and I are starting to feel good again, lying on a black sand beach in the warm Mediterranean sun. I decide to walk the beach. As I'm walking, this cute tan blond is really checking me out, then the guy she's with starts staring at me too, and then I'm running, and its Jen and Toph and only a thousand islands with a million beaches but a very small world. So we moved into their apartment on the beach for five dollars a night, and have been having a joyous reunion.

We've been here a week, and the sun has been generously coloring our pale bodies to a more suitable shade. Toph looks like he's Greek, and Jen is a goddess. We have been eating our meals on the patio and sleeping with the doors open. We are having a small celebration, for we are leaving tonight to begin the trek back to Athens, over to Brindisi, up to Heidelberg for a night, and then flying out of Frankfurt. I missed my ticketed flight days ago, but I'm sure they'll put me on standby as soon as they can. The last thing United Airlines needs is a bearded wanderer parked in front of their ticket counter.

My European tour has come to an end, and I am both saddened and excited about going home. I am excited about my family and friends, next semester at Pepperdine, about life and youth that slips away even as I write. I am excited at the sound of gulls and the sun sparkling off a clear blue sea. I love. I live. I laugh. Is it possible to be more blessed? I wonder.

But right now the waters Odysseus sailed call to me emphatically, and I feel it's only polite to slip myself into their loving embraces.

So, this Euro-tour comes to a close, but the story continues, and grows more joyous daily. And I continue to wonder. And appreciate

you citizen of this old town
 or pilgrim from far away
looking for some
tranquility
here you may become silent
 at the well of all beauty
and life
no one is a stranger
in this old church
where God as a loving father
is waiting
only for you
—*ANONYMOUS*
Bruge, Belgium

WANDERLUST TENANT #1

Notice Things.

The very first tenant of belief in the theory of Wanderlust Appreciation is that you have to Notice Things. You don't even have to go anywhere to practice this tenant. Wherever you are is a gift.

Beauty surrounds, even in the oddest, most sterile places. If you're eyes aren't open, you will never learn to live a life of appreciation, no matter where you go. If you're eyes are open, you will never stop. Notice things. Butterflies. Streaks of cloud in the skyscape. The breeze as it moves the wooden chimes, or the smell of rain on the warm asphalt. There are a host of things to notice, even on the most familiar pathways. Notice them. And in doing so, you remain open to wonder.

"If you remain open to wonder, your heart can breathe."
—*JAPHY TINYSPEAR*

"Cathy, I'm lost," I said, though I knew she was sleeping. "I'm empty and aching and I don't know why." Counting the cars on the New Jersey turnpike, they've all gone to look for America.
—*PAUL SIMON*, "America"

PILGRIMAGE

AMERICA

TWO

JUNE 21

Victorville, California

6:21 a.m. Been riding the Shadow two hours. Right now I'm sitting in the early morning sunshine in the AmPm parking lot off of Bear Valley on I15. The dreams and plans of a year have today been realized. It was cold, much colder than I remember it being in June, and I was in my jacket hunched low over the engine trying to stay warm. It did not help. The cold made my eyes bleed tears and run little rivers of salt joy back toward my ears, where they were whipped free of my face by the wind. I rode alone. Climbing free of the basin toward the high desert, I was blinded by the sun's first showing. Literally blinded, with eyes full of tears, the world became dazzling, and I pulled over briefly to dry my eyes and fish sunglasses from my pack. The desert has a corner on a lonely type of beauty, especially at dawn's first light, before the heat grows. Now I thaw in the gentle caress of the sun, aided by twenty ounces of murky motor oil java that couldn't taste better. Toph will join me here presently. We're looking for America.

Later. We pounded the highway hard today. Toph joined me at the Summit Inn and we flew north. We stopped above Vegas for a late

afternoon lunch from Toph's cardboard pantry that he has rigged behind his seat. We ate beans from the can, and bread. We dusted our water bottles. And then, in the middle of nowhere, with not a shade tree in sight, we napped. Tactical Error #1. We woke up parched. Our lips were cracked. Both of us bleary from the discomfort of napping in 112 degree heat, we packed up in silence and drove north, looking for relief. We pulled off in the Valley of Fire, which was ironically appropriate given the hell we were in.

We found a general store. And we raided the refrigerated drinks ... gulping gallons of Gatorade and purchasing enough water to cross the desert in a covered wagon. Yes, we are stupid, but we can be taught.

JUNE 22
Durango, Colorado

I sit in a green valley in God's country, outside Durango, and I am happy. I am also saturated with fatigue, for the last two days have seen many miles. Toph joined me in Victorville, and we cruised the Las Vegas desert together up to St. George. I hooked a right on Highway 9 to Kanub (Toph was heading north to go through Denver for a Jen-visit), where I spent one starlit night. Right before I went to sleep, I had a cigarette. I recently finished *Still Life with a Woodpecker* by Robbins, which inspired me to start smoking on this trip. I think it's cool to watch people smoke. It's a James Dean thing. I even like the smell of the Camel hardpack that I purchased to learn with. The problem is this: I can't do it. I cough and hack like Tuberculosis incarnate. It is ridiculous. Plus, I woke up this morning, and my breath tasted like I'd gargled with manure. So I think I'll cut my losses and call it quits. And spare myself the joy of blacklung.

Today the ride was okay until I hit Cortez. Then, I was amazed. Awestruck. The mountains and the valleys and the green of the hills and trees were symphony and majesty to my tired soul. That breeze of glory carried my horse and I to Durango, where I now prepare to bed for the evening. A dog barks; the sun sets; I hear children laughing in the distance. I am, like all my fellow journeymen, a wanderer in this pilgrimage of life.

A dog named Boo just became my friend. He is black and white, and when I scratch him behind the ears, he becomes satisfaction visible.

JUNE 23
Garden City, Kansas

I write by candlelight in my tent outside of Garden City, Kansas. Today it seemed I rode a million miles. While crossing the desert valley of San Luis, I nearly dozed, so I pulled off and threw myself in the sand and napped in the noon-day heat. I slept until a very concerned lady screeched to a halt and bawled, "Are you OKAY? Are you OKAY?" When I raised my head, she seemed disappointed. She

said, "You should go find some shade to nap in," and I answered in a parched murmur, "There is no shade."

I'm a tad embarrassed about what happened last night. I almost burned Durango down. I was set up to sleep comfortably, on a hillside, with incredibly tall, dry grass surrounding my makeshift camp. I was a little nervous to start a blaze (I was trying to heat my chili) because I didn't want to catch the surrounding grass on fire. I thought to myself, if only I had a fire-ring ... made of rocks, the guts of an abandoned washing machine, anything. As I poked around the hillside, I found exactly what I needed ... the perfect firebreak, round and everything. Tactical Error #2. It was an old tire. There is a problem with using this as a fire-ring, but I didn't realize it until about five minutes later, when my little fire was crackling nicely within the old tire. It was then that the old tire began to crackle nicely as well. Silly, silly, Mike! And the flames rose up to almost my height (which I guess isn't really that high), and the black, noxious smoke billowed. Not knowing what else to do, I poured my water bottle on the fire and blew on it as hard as I could. It didn't really help. Thankfully, there were walkers nearby who spotted the fire, and soon a foul-mouthed dad came charging over with a fire extinguisher and some choice words about my intelligence.

Some people are so unfriendly. I packed up my stuff in silence, and
as I rode away, I could hear the wail of fire engines coming to ensure
that my stupidity was contained, which it was. Now the arsonist sleeps
wrapped in his chagrin.

This morning's ride from Durango to Wolf Creek was beautiful
but bitter cold. I awoke wrapped in frost. That was not in the original
conception of the tour.

Today I raced a storm front. The 10 East to La Junta is seventy miles
of loneliness, and I let out a whoop, opened the throttle, and raced
against the heavens, for a drop of rain shatters skin like a bullet. Today
I did not lose.

It is hard to understand the reason insects continue to fly over
highways. There is an abundance of peril-free living space on either
side of the road, yet a host today have perished to my thunderstick, my
jacket, and my forehead.

A man named Homer gave me a brochure for the Christian
Motorcyclists Association. Their motto is, "There's still time to change
the road you're on," which is a line from Zepplin's "Stairway." In a live
recording of that song, Robert Plant sings the lyric, and then in the
pause afterward says, "I hope so."

You and me both, Rob.

JUNE 24
Hutchinson, Kansas

I lie on a bed, and a ceiling fan blows cool air onto my warm body. I am at my grandparents' house. Here there is love, peace, cleanliness, and laughter. I am sleepy and clean.

Tonight my grandma served the tastiest meal. It was homemade chicken noodle stew served over mashed potatoes with homegrown green beans and pickled beets. For desert she served a banana crème pie prepared with her world-famous crust. I am content.

Hutchinson is America. The summer nights are warm and fragrant. The sky is filled with stars, mosquitoes, and the song of crickets. Life, and America, clings to your sticky skin on these warm summer nights. The breeze sighs quietly and rocks me gently to sleep

Celestial
the patterns of glide,
of circle
of orbit
of grace
slow moving and methodical:
dust in the sunlight

As twilight deepened into night, and the luminous blue of the sky absorbed the silhouette blackness of trees and houses and grain elevators, I sat still on my grandma's porch. I felt a prompting to move, to seek friendship. I rode my bike down East Carpenter toward Main. As I approached Main, another bike swung into view. It was Toph, who had been riding hard from Colorado, where his true love lives. He was weary, but in the darkness of a Kansas night, his smile was wide. Something about reuniting with a good friend across the miles speaks loudly to my soul.

JUNE 25
Hutchinson, Kansas

It is over one hundred degrees today. Grandpa, Toph, and I just got back from the farm my parents own outside of town. I can't believe how run down it is. With care it could be a wonderful corner of the world, but now it is just a depressing hole. I'd like to live there, to make it match my visions, yet it will take time, effort, money, and commitment. So I lack a few things. Sometimes I see incredible potential here, sometimes incredible stagnation.

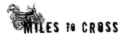

I vow to avoid stagnation.

Another warm summer evening. I sit on the front porch swing and rock in the moonlight, listening to the chorus of insects. Now that Toph has joined me, we will journey onward together. In the dusk I take a ride. I go out to South Hutch and around to Washboard Avenue, through the golf course and park to the baseball diamond. The lights are on (day had again faded), and the game is near its conclusion. I park my bike in the grass there, walk up to the fence, and inhale deeply. The fresh cut grass and the brick dust infield and the uniforms and the crowd and the scoreboard all flood my soul. As I watch, the final out is made, and the players line up and shake hands with the other team. I ride home then full of nostalgia and happiness. My thunderhorse understands, and we hum the same sad tune on the way.

JUNE 26
Hutchinson, Kansas

Tonight my thoughts vanish as I raise the pen. It is late, and Toph and I have yet to succumb to slumber. Tomorrow we leave Hutch for Oklahoma City and my Auntie Kay's.

By the way, Toph was excited at the potential of our farm. The place definitely has an abundance of potential. I love the land. I love the smells of the country, the sound of wind through the trees, the beauty of well-tended earth. Nature. It feeds the soul. Maybe I should become a farmer. Or just be rich enough to own an estate like the Huntington Gardens.

JUNE 28
Edmond, Oklahoma

Yesterday was my mother's birthday. Yesterday we drove from Hutch to my Auntie Kay's farmhouse in Edmond. Last night was a warm evening with a cool breeze and a full moon and a hundred fluttering bats and a thousand fireflies, and we sat on the porch and listened. We listened to the rustle of the trees and the song of crickets. Yesterday we went swimming in the pond.

We met Dean here, and now at last the three American journeymen are united. We have all traveled in Europe together (Dean and I traveled to Budapest and Bern together), and now we will cruise America.

Today it is hot. I sit on the meadow with my back to the sun as I write. A stray cloud passes in front of the sun, the breeze picks up, and I am cooled.

I love my Auntie Kay. Her spirit is so young and fresh that it uplifts me; I laugh with her continually. I love the friendship that she and my mom share. It seems that we get wearied by life, yet friendship and laughter erase wrinkles and restore youth.

JUNE 29
Lake Keystone, Oklahoma

The sun is gone, music plays indoors, friends and relatives are all around, my skin feels smooth and tight, and I am tired and happy, for today has been spent at the lake. After dinner we walked through a green secluded meadow to a little pond, and we skipped stones in the twilight. This morning we said goodbye to May and Auntie Kay, and then for the first time we all hit the highway together. Now we rest at Lake Keystone. The family is well; my grandma and grandpa, Chad (a cousin), and Lexi (another cousin) are great. I can hear my grandad's laugh roll through the evening. He has a great laugh. It is a barrel

laugh that only a rascal like him can make innocent; it sparks other
fires of laughter wherever it lights.

The night has begun, and I will go enjoy, lest the opportunity be
lost forever.

JUNE 30
Lake Keystone, Oklahoma

Today is a lazy day. We slept too late and drank too much coffee
and ate too much breakfast and became, as my grandma might say,
"plum tuckered." Toph naps, and Dean and I are still as we pen a few
words for posterity. Outside, the afternoon jaunt to the lake is being
prepared. I think I shall go lend a hand, or at least a helpful comment
or two.

Later: The day has passed in a glory of sunshine and water and
laughter. I have three mosquito bites, and my skin tone leans a bit
to the red shade; nonetheless I prepare my bed with a smile. My
grandmother said that this morning she and Toph shared the porch
for a little time of quiet. She said it "did her heart good" to see Toph
praising the "man upstairs." Toph and I have gone back and forth
talking about his faith. While I concede that his faith is a benefit to

him, and that his quality of life is greater because of it, I also find that there are parts of the Christian format that are truly difficult for me to come to terms with. The concept of hell, the stark reality of so much pain and suffering in this world ... and even the crux of the faith centered on a crucified savior ... these things to me are mountain-sized obstacles. I believe there is a Creator, and I believe at the core there is love. But it sure is difficult to move from the great mystery into what happens on the corner church every Sunday morning.

So for now I know I don't need to know. This pilgrim is content to appreciate life. In the duration, I'll offer eternal praises to the One who is for eternity. The sounds of the night are songs of thankfulness, and I join in with glad heart and bright eye. Beyond this, who can plumb the mystery?

JULY 2
Outside of Hot Springs, Arkansas

Toph and I are awake this early morning, on a mountainside that overlooks a lush green valley and the wide Arkansas river. Yesterday morning we said goodbye to my grandparents at the lake and headed east. We stopped for a long afternoon in Kingston Arkansas, off the 412 and 21. We ate and dozed, and I read a bit of Tolkien in the Valley Café off the town square. Then we journeyed until dark, and made camp, and slept fitfully throughout the warm, humid night.

The sun has just crept above the ridge of trees to the east, and already it is hot. Toph, like the zealot he is, does sit ups; Dean sleeps on.

JULY 4
New Orleans, Louisiana

I just woke up on the floor of a brick house in a nice little neighborhood in the outskirts of New Orleans (New Orlin, I think is the local pronunciation, although it's hard to understand a majority of what's said) in the state of Louisiana in this great nation called America.

last twilight
walking on a path deserted,
my eyes dazzled by the contrast
between silhouettes
and light faded,
so that when I glanced
along the darkened path
the shapes and vague movements...
ghostlike
were unreal
images cast from older days:
a country lad's daydreams,
remembrances
of a more innocent age.
The songs of locust blanketed me
wave after wave; I heard
hoof-clops of a rider returning
from a general store supply run, perhaps,
and I imagined,
giddy, like a schoolgirl
after her love's kindness,
fireflies, and a soft harmonica
playing on the edge of memory.

it was a helicopter,
not a firefly,
and I realized that
the hum of harp
was the tollroad speeding cars
at breakneck speeds
toward progress.

JULY 5
Gulf Shores, Alabama

Tonight we are driving around Gulf Shores, Alabama, and the rain is just pouring down, and we have no place to stay. I'm thinking, *This is an adventure. It sucks, but that's what happens with tricky things like adventures.* The two campgrounds in town are full (and soaked); the hotels have no vacancies, for it is the Fourth of July weekend. Yet we three young explorers continue on, neither hopeful nor hopeless, into the bleary night. We come to our fifth church of the evening, Our Lady of the Gulf. No cars, but a light is on in the very back corner. Dean knocks on the door, and Father O'Neil's smile is seen across the parking lot. His laughter is music; his heart is gold. We follow Father O'Neil to a separate cottage where CCD is held weekly. He unlocks the door, and we step in out of the rain. Tonight we have a warm, dry, safe place to sleep because of his kindness. We have food and drink (chips and beer, but it is enough) thanks to his generosity.

Now I glance up at a picture of Christ on the wall, and my heart in its involuntary pit-a-patter dances and laughs and praises its Creator. (At this juncture in my spiritual quest, God looks like a personal Creator who is actively involved. Perhaps Christ was on to something, perhaps not. But I am fascinated by the halo-ed serenity that adorns

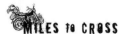

cathedral and CCD room alike. As for what it would take for me to bend the knee, I have no idea. I definitely believe in a good designer, because there is too much good in the design. Joseph Heller rages against this, and rages against "phlegm" as his example, but it is easy to see the design in it. It is we human dolts who bring the ugliness. The beauty stands objectively.) Our wet clothes hang about the room in a fruitless effort to dry. I attempt to color in the rather bald spots in my journal entries.

On the second, we spent the night in a trailer in the Louisiana swamp fourteen miles west of Winnfield. We went to the Baptist church there, and Dean found us a place in a brave high school student's doublewide trailer home. The next day, we hit New Orleans and stayed with Angele. We had a blast. The city was amazing, the hospitality was excellent, and our tour guide was a hotty. The city threw a raging party for the fourth. We saw the place almost at its peak, and what a crazy peak it is. We wandered into a magic shop on Bourbon Street that held something unholy. For an extra two bucks we could have gone in the back room to see this thing—whatever it was. The evil was so thick in that place that I would have paid a hundred times that just to pass on that opportunity. There are some crazy things going down in New Orlin.

Our travels have been full of surprise. I'm surprised by beauty. I'm

surprised by joy. I think a lot when I drive. I feel a lot. I dream. It's good.

JULY 7
Atlanta, Georgia

Rain. Rain. Rain. Wet. Everything is wet. Yesterday it rained down upon our heads from 9 a.m. to 6 p.m. We had coffee and eggs and grits at Bills Fine Foods Café and left puddles on the floor. We reached Atlanta late and slept gloriously late in the morning. Today we saw the Atlanta Underground and a three-story tribute to Coca-Cola.

The afternoon and evening have melted into the past, and my eyes are heavy as I write. Dean and Toph plan tomorrow's ride. Our hosts here have been wonderful. This evening we visited Stone Mountain State Park and watched the laser light show there, and saw the Dixieland flag waving proudly, which caused me to pause. That didn't make sense to me, and it still doesn't. Can you keep the pride of place and lose the love of hatred? I hope so.

JULY 9
Smokey Mountains, North Carolina

Morning. The sunlight filters down through green leaves, and there is a smell of campfire in the air. I share a lonely breakfast with nature as I write. Peanut butter, bread, apple, and water. My friends, myself, and this forest are in North Carolina. A swallow sits on Toph's mirror and shrieks his delight to the woods that surround. Last night with Keystone and campfire, Dean, Toph, and I shared stories (we are all writing novels in our minds as we drive. In mine, *Brilliant Young Psychos*, the protagonists are all bandits, genius-thieves. The last scene is the slow-motion death of the most likeable brilliant young psycho, a police officer chasing him on motorcycle, and he skids around a mountainous curve and vaults beyond the edge, to Pink Floyd's "Goodbye Cruel World" from *The Wall* album. This is important) and a sense of well-being and where we were and where we were headed. I pause to prepare another peanut butter sandwich. As I sit, a spider wanders upon my leg, and I feel obliged to speed

his journey with a flick of my forefinger. I look across the glade at the three machines that brought us here. My '84 Shadow 750, black and chrome. It looks the outlaw. Toph's Magna, maroon, custom seat, windshield; his is the standard tour bike. Dean's got a Yamaha 500, red, which continually amazes with its power and tenacity. The other day someone asked Dean where he lived, and he, in mock-seriousness, answered, "The road is my home; my bike is my house." I think bike is art. Curves, lines, shape; it has technological beauty. When we ride, it, like the swallow on Toph's mirror, shrieks its delight to the woods that surround.

Evening. A long ride today. We visited Sliding Rock, and slid down this behemoth rock in the middle of a river. Then we cruised the Blue Ridge Parkway for hours and hours. At Hickory we stopped at an old fashioned Dairy Queen, and the ladies behind the counter told us we looked like Calvin Klein models. That was a slight ego boost. Then we rode and rode and rode, until we arrived in Chapel Hill outside Durham. Here we stay with the mother of a friend of Dean's. The laughter still comes, but sometimes it gets buried in fatigue.

My rear is burning. I crapped fire today. I never realized what four thousand miles would do to my colon. I need some Chapstick or something. I might split in two.

JULY 10
Chapel Hill, North Carolina

The day dawns early, and we rise and ride forth to meet it. We prepare to leave Chapel Hill. We seek. We journey to an America that exists only in the past, through the lens of nostalgia. It is not a geographical search; rather, it is a spiritual quest for regained youth, innocence, vigor. "Ride, boldly ride," the Shade replied, "If you seek for El Dorado."

I'm realizing that a motorcycle is a means of transcendental transport. I'm sure this is some sort of kickback memory from *Zen and the Art of Motorcycle Maintenance*, which did inspire this trip over a year ago. But wherever it came from, it's true. In a real sense, one's being is hurled unprotected through space at massive speeds, and death lies in someone's blind spot. There is the hum of the bike and the roar of the wind and the knowledge that death is an instant. Yet the soul, in the face of death, takes wing, and soars and laughs. In the instant, all perceptions change—the potential for excitement is at its maxim. The green of the hills causes giddiness; the wind in the face intoxicates. The mundane becomes thrilling. On a motorcycle, you are transported to an experience of life that is breathless. It is the perfect vehicle for pilgrimage.

JULY 11
Virginia Beach, Virginia

We arrived in Virginia Beach yesterday in the pouring rain, and jumped straight into the shower. We are staying with Dean's family: his sister, brother-in-law, nephew, and niece, with visits from his mom. All are fun, and high energy. Last night we watched *Easy Rider*. The acid scene was way too tripped out, and I almost left the room. One thing Jack said that made sense is that when people see true freedom, it makes them scared. And when people get scared, they get dangerous. This could be universally true. It happened to a young Jack Nicholson in the movie.

It happened to Martin Luther King, Jr. It happened to a young Nazarene. A life unfettered both inspires and terrifies.

Today we picked blueberries—buckets and buckets of the things, and it was like finding nuggets of gold. Dean's nephew and niece were classic, squealing, "Here's one! Here's one!" when there were thousands about.

We visited the Atlantic. I body surfed and caught a jellyfish in my pocket. We ate oyster on the half-shell and drank Coronas. We have wandered from sea to shining sea. I think a lot about what I'm doing and why I'm doing it. I'm looking for something within me by putting miles on my bike. I know this doesn't make sense, but it's not a bad idea either. So, no answers yet, but all thoughts are positive. No doubt that this Freedom Tour shreds all over *Easy Rider*. Comparisons are odious, says Kerouac, and of course he's right. However, let's be honest. *Easy Rider* starts and ends in illegitimacy. Fonda's dismissal of their trip at the end proves it. Even he knew they were wasting space, wasting time. Even he knew there was more to life than money and pleasure, and yet he gave no answers. I say it is significance. I want to live a life that is significant—to leave something behind that is good, worthy, lasting, maybe even inspiring. What is my legacy? What is my contribution? How can my life matter?

In Bunn, North Carolina, we three roadsters purchased small American flags for one dollar each. They are mounted on our bikes with pride.

Of course I've found the quality known as America. It's everywhere I turn.

JULY 12
Virginia Beach, Virginia

Oil change for the transports, and Krispy Kreme for the transported. We time traveled to Colonial Williamsburg and consumed some stout colonial ale. We strolled around William and Mary, with its stately brick buildings and well-tended grounds and sighed. Our history seems young, and unreal. I'm referring, of course, to the history of America, as opposed to the history of Europe. And I suppose I'm referring to the history of the West Coast as opposed to the Colonies. Stately Pepperdine, which my heart has taken as its own, is the stucco and tile majesty erected with care over the last forty years. I love

California, but there is a clamor within me for the history, poetry, and beauty of the ages. But not a loud enough clamor, I guess, to cause me to move.

JULY 13
Virginia Beach, Virginia

Last night there was a small birthday celebration held in honor of my twenty-first. I was quite touched. We played an enthusiastic game of Trivial Pursuit. There was much laughter, there were many smiles, and a good time was had by all.

Dean's nephew, after watching Disney's animated *Robin Hood*, looked up at me with total sincerity and asked me if Robin Hood used a stunt double, or if he did the stunts all by himself. I told him I didn't know the answer to that question, and I don't.

Today we are going to splash in the Atlantic. Dean, Toph, and I were discussing how we envisioned this summer to be an exodus from the reality we know into the unknown of America. The problem is that America has little of the unknown about it. There are no castles to explore, just another IHOP. It is impossible for us to leave behind the reality we know because all throughout the nation, the same reality exists. America exists in the eyes of those we meet. In the local color of phrases and accents. We smell it in the food, and in the sticky heat of the highway. It is good. Not unknown ... but close and unfamiliar.

Tomorrow we are going to Quantico, to visit my old high school, to stir the bittersweet cup of my memory. My dad is a lieutenant colonel in the Marine Corps, and when I was a freshman in high school, he was transferred here for a year. I learned a ton in Quantico. I learned how to use my will to be a force on the football field. I learned a lot about lust. I tried very hard to learn about sex, but could find no willing teachers. I witnessed several fistfights, and engaged in one or two myself. I learned that the best form of defense is a life that flies under the radar, but if that ultimately fails, then it is best to strike hard and fast. Maybe I didn't learn really learn that ... maybe I just wrote it to sound tough. Maybe my visit to Quantico High School is to see if, in my heart, the friends that I made there were real, if the terror I felt upon arrival was real, and if the year itself that rocketed past, in

MILES to CROSS

the midst of sport and hormone and confusion, was real. It is hard to decide if I was more lost then, or now.

JULY 16
Brooklyn Heights, New York City

D.C. to Maryland, to Delaware, to Pennsylvania, to New Jersey, to New York City, and finally, to Cyndi's apartment. Toph is playing guitar next to me as pasta cooks on the stove. The states we traversed yesterday drifted by and melted away under the dry brick sun. Cyndi (the Cyndi who still drives me crazy because I still think that dating her would be like holding hands with the wind) wore my leather vest and rode on the back of my hog and wrapped her arms around me tight, and I became high, and secure; and my tires touched not the pavement as we roared and flew. Shirts boiled in the wind, and we lived our freedom.

Backtrack a couple of days: The Capitol with cool yuppies of the political sphere and a call to Cyndi that brings her to Washington. We see the sights, tour the capital, rearrange our packs to accommodate her on my bike, and blaze—to Plainsfield, New Jersey, to see Toph's Aunt Donna and Uncle Bruce, the most awesome New Age feminist and mystic philosopher I have ever met. They both teach at Rutgers. Their daughter (Toph's cousin) sings Opera in the city, and I've heard her present Hendel's *Messiah* as a form of grace to a jaded world.

5:45 a.m. I wake and cruise Cyndi to the city. We eat lunch at Sal's Atlantic Café on Atlantic Street, Brooklyn. I shook Sal's hand and made a friend. Sal served us ice cream. Very energetic, he was, with arm hair leaping off his forearm as if manic—not that he had an overabundance of hair on his arm, simply an unusual example of hair distancing itself as starkly as possible from its place of origin.

Toph and Mike showed up at 3 p.m., and we rushed to a taping of *David Letterman*. It was pretty funny, but I always leave those things with a headache and an anxiety complex that the star is bipolar, unable to exist outside of the role. Like Holden Caufield, all that laughter and poise depresses me.

Van Morrison sings in the other room, and a quarter moon rises over lower Manhattan. I ready myself to legally open a Heineken,

and the toast will be to the Lord of the natural and the Lord of the manmade. The cat's name is Emerson. I love cats. If it scratches me, it dies.

Toph said tonight that the Lord embraces us on the earth with the wind and the waters. Tonight, Toph is wise beyond his years. This would be a great moment, except that I'm digging Cyndi and thinking that she's digging Dean.

What a screwed up thing insecurity is.

JULY 17
Brooklyn Heights, New York City

The Lady of Liberty stares fixedly out to sea, but as I lean and write, I'm sure she steals a glance in my direction, and a smile may even flash across her stoic face as she contemplates the small rider on the rooftop in Brooklyn Heights. We walked around Manhattan today. Perused the Metropolitan Museum of Art. Bought a dog from a vendor in Central Park. I made a friend in Central Park, but it turned out that he just wanted to expose himself in front of me, so that friendship didn't really go anywhere. We walked to Union Square.

I'd describe New York as too much and too many. Too many people, too many buildings, too much traffic, too much noise. Too much misery. On the Subway to the Met, an old woman shouted incomprehensible convictions with dusty voice and varied enthusiastic gestures. The man across the car was continually shifting positions and muttering and clinching his fists and his teeth. It looked like he was going to combust. He muttered filth, and it was frightening.

Before I got here, I thought I wanted to be here. Now that I'm here, I know I want to leave. The skyscrapers of Manhattan cast a shadow that rests upon my soul. As we walked today, I saw much and said little. My mind was thick with the burden of thought, but nothing clear and no conclusions. When needs multifarious confront, I get weary. We rode the elevator to the top of the World Trade Center. From that height, the city looks friendlier. But even then I was scanning the horizon for the beginning of what's next.

I want to ride.

Sage and I occasionally still spend time together when we are both home from school. I spoke with her last night on the phone, and missed her.

JULY 20
Brooklyn Heights, New York City

Today I saw the dream. It is the dream of every capitalist, every American, every human being conscious enough to see that it is money that greases the gears of life: the twin estates of a Pepperdine

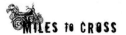

friend, complete with courtyard and guesthouse and pool and dock and boat and jet ski, in the green New England town of Darien, Connecticut. The possibilities are vast. I've seen the prize. I simply have no idea how to get there. Our state lottery system is so fickle. We took his boat across the sound over to Long Island, and beached it there. I confess, I felt just like Gatsby ... just lacking his charm, money, good looks, and wit. Other than that, just like Gatsby.

JULY 21

Brooklyn Heights, New York City

Tomorrow we leave the city. Despite the heat, insecurity, and temporary angst, New York has truly been an amazing stop. *Cats* and Cyndi and the skyline and the rooftop and fire escape and hot sticky nights and lasagna and Chinese and the subway and Darien and the wealth we saw there and music and beer and friends all melted into one incredible time. A backrub and a glass of wine have made me thoughtful, but sleepy. Toph and Dean prepare to journey. There is some soft conversation in the kitchen. I am warm, happy, healthy, and

well-fed, which is good, considering I'm traveling. The city shines on into the night. I look out upon the city and I sigh; it is time to leave. The open country beckons with a breeze, and my heart is light as I answer the call to venture. We rise with the dawn to ride. I am glad.

JULY 25
Richmond, New Hampshire

In front of me lies a map of the United States, and on it I have traced our journey thus far. The distance we have come, and the distance we have yet to go, are overwhelming. I pause to fill my cup with coffee and to listen to the sounds of this New Hampshire farmhouse. The house is creaking and huge, and right now I sit in its country-style kitchen and watch a white, long-haired kitten swat and gnaw playfully at a rubber band she found. The cat's name is Cosmos. The kitchen she is filling with her rumbling belongs to our friend Tommi, a travelling friend from Heidelberg. The day is cloudy, and the crickets outside sing of the approaching rain.

The past few days have been filled with brooding—thick, wonderful New England. We have traveled through Mystic, Newport, and Boston. We tarried at Harvard, and the actual institution, when compared to my mental picture of it, caused disappointment. During a season of flirtation with playing football there, I spent much energy chatting up the coach, lifting record amounts (for me, that is), and thrilled about the prospect of a degree from Harvard. Disappointment weighs heavy on the pride. If I hadn't received their letter denying me admittance, our stop at Harvard would have been painted in all sorts of brighter colors.

We spent a night near Portland, Maine, with Becky Smith's parents. It was crisp and salty as we unloaded our bikes in the dark, and we couldn't see beyond the yard. We woke up early and saw white lighthouses in the bright morning sun. New England houses and barns nestled among green trees with glimpses of the sparkling cold ocean filled me with joy. We stopped at New Orchard beach and spent a few hours in the blazing sun, until our skin felt tight, clean, and good, like it's supposed to during the summer. No sign of Jaws.

We drove through a green, empty New Hampshire to this

farmhouse in Richmond. The kitten is relatively quiet as she cleans herself in the corner. The rain hasn't started, but it smells very near. I fold my map and hear the song of robins. It's a good song. I take a deep breath of this country air, I feel and I listen, and I am satisfied.

Tommie's aunt lives alone in a haunted country inn. We visited her yesterday. The inn is over a hundred years old, and has a very colorful history, which includes spending some time as a brothel. But the hair stood up on my neck as Tommie's aunt told us her ghost stories. Once, several years earlier, she had just gotten into bed, when she thought she heard a horse and buggy pull up the round circular entrance. She wondered at this, when she heard the front door open, and people walked in talking and laughing. This obviously frightened her, so she prepared herself as best as she could, as if someone was breaking into her home. She listened as she heard footsteps and voices climb the creaking stairs and walk down the hall. She heard a bedroom door open, and then shut. After an eternity of gathering courage, she followed the voices to see if anyone was there. Nobody was, of course. The pounding in her ears must have been her heart.

JULY 27
Trenton, Ontario

Yesterday, like so many other days, bleared its way into the past. Unlike so many other days, it saw three bikers wander into a Ben & Jerry's Ice Cream Factory and devour complimentary pints of Chunky Monkey, Cherry Garcia, and Heath Bar Crunch. It saw three cold and wet explorers travel two hundred fifty miles through grand, green, and wet country. It introduced them to Bill the Hippie. He gave us a warm place to stay and a beer or two. We woke up to cats and kids and the smell of piss and vomit, for Bill was a hippie, and his house was like a commune. The experience was unique, interesting, and paints a more authentic picture of the Grateful Dead phenomenon.

We have made camp for the night in a secluded wooded area sixty miles east of Toronto. The sun is setting, and when the light fades, we will start a fire. It will be cold tonight.

My thoughts tonight are of warm and peaceful times. This tour is an amazing, exhausting adventure, but tonight I drift off the pleasures of

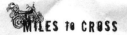

normalcy. My friends and I share exhaustion as we share laughter. It is quiet now. The light fades, and we make ready for the night.

AUGUST 1
Brainard, Minnesota

Today, in Brainard, Minnesota, we water skied on glass. William Van Dyke, a roommate from Heidelberg, has taken us into his grandparents' estate on Gull Lake within the cradle of affluence. I slip into that cradle with ease.

Detroit, Chicago, Milwaukee, St. Paul, and Minneapolis have all blown by like leaves in the wake of my motorcycle. In my mind, I can see various skylines, hear traffic, and smell and taste multiple air pollutants. In reality, I hear the sounds of the lake, the song of crickets, the silence of the trees.

My heart is heavy, and I don't know why. My soul feels sick today. Toph sees that I'm down, and it frustrates him. I think it's a mixture of insecurity, loneliness, and a sense of being lost. I'm still having fun with my buddies, but sometimes the peace is elusive.

I wonder
about a lot of things
and there is a sadness.
I am only guessing

but I think it is
the sadness of
authenticity.

No wonder
It's
So
rare.

I'm absolute BS, by the way. I'd like to think that I'm the real one, morally superior because I'm the authentic one. But the reality is that I'm a cheap façade like everyone else. At times, I'm more bitter perhaps, because I'm not really very good at hiding my brokenness behind polite chit-chat. I am a hypocrite, unsettled at my brokenness, and petrified that people will discover how false I really am, how vain, how shallow, how greedy. I am a FAKE, but even more emasculated than the typical fake because I covet the ability to be proudly false. I condemn the role-play in others, and am terrified of it in myself. I don't have any idea what this all means, or really how to change it.

If only I could stop masturbating.

AUGUST 5
Alsada, Montana

There is so much space here in Montana, and so much healthy loneliness that my heart rejoices as I glide, and joins the clouds and hills in praise. We have stopped for breakfast in Alzada and have filled ourselves with eggs, toast, hash browns, and coffee. America does breakfast right.

We have traveled long since Van Dyke's place in Brainard. We ate supper on the third in Salem, South Dakota, and watched the town cruise Main, flip a U, and cruise it again. We slept in a field and witnessed a truly majestic sunset followed by a glorious sunrise. We rode to Rushmore. Pictures cannot tell the story of a living mountain molded in stately respect to the men who molded a living nation. Eyes shine with wonder.

There is a Harley Davidson rally taking place in Sturgis. The past two days have seen bikers and bikes in their glory and their shame.

We met Rick The Lonely Biker, and he rode with us to Sturgis. It was a Dead show on wheels; the whole thing danced in leather and otherworldliness. It was amazing, oddly beautiful, and frightening. We left within the hour (afraid our imported bikes would cause offense).

Somewhere in the quiet darkness of Wyoming, we slept. The myriad of stars laughed and twinkled at us in the moonless night. We heard the howl and bark of coyotes, but none approached the still, road–

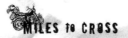

weary travelers or their resting horses.

AUGUST 9

Rimrock, Washington

The past three days, we have laughed about Ghormley Meadow. It is a retreat off of Highway 12 west of Yakima, and the place is crawling with goodness. Toph and I worked here as Maintenance MEN one summer previous, and so this is a reprieve from my angst (which lingers in the wings like shadow). These three days have been a waltz of joy, and the colors and emotions have blurred into one beautiful memory.

We prepare to leave and travel south along the coast. Home in a few days and a thousand miles. Yet Ghormley feels like home, and my heart is heavy as I pack my things.

AUGUST 12

Mission Viejo, California

Three days hard travel down the coast. Our first was a great night of firelight, cheap beer, and apple liquor in South Newport, Oregon. We woke up to clouds off the ocean, and the smell of salt. As we traveled south, the weather temp increased, and so did my sense of the summer's waning. The desert clime of the Bakersfield valley only helped to send my soul into some wasteland of its own devising. We officially ended the Tour on the pier of Alice's Restaurant in Malibu, which is also where we each had worked this year as busboys to save money for our trip. I returned to my parents' house just past midnight.

the sun shines bright
this morning
quiet
Saturday
I'm thinking of a lot of things
but not much of anything
at all.

like a flea
being sought by the wandering
scratch of a dog,
irritated,
or a fly
buzzing the ear of a picnic practitioner
to distraction,
the poetry of discontent goads
not to despair
but rather
to annoying hopefullness
holding out to the end
that true balm does exist:
contentment,
rest.
only not here.

Today the Freedom Tour is past tense.

A dream realized is sadness.

Unlike the Grecian Urn, the ecstasy is felt and slips away into rainy day memories.

John Denver breaks my heart as I try to keep freedom and America alive in my mind.

Outside rain sprinkles down, and inside my brother naps on the living room couch.

It's good to be home, I suppose.

WANDERLUST TENANT #2

Know Yourself.

The second tenant of this Wanderlust Appreciation belief is that whoever you are is a gift. You are beautiful right now, just as you are, incredibly more beautiful than you think you are. If our media culture would just keep its mitts out of our self-consciousness, you would discover this. You are loved, right now, just as you are. You are loved beyond your ability to comprehend. And the great news, the hope that rises as bright as the sun, is that you are a work in progress. Notice things. Know yourself. Unless you spend the time it takes to know yourself, you will continue to project your own issues on the people that surround you, or sometimes even the places in which you find yourself. You can change your surroundings ... the people and the places. But you can't travel away from you. In order to know yourself, you have to listen to your emptiness, to your dissatisfaction, to your restlessness. It is telling you something about your heart's deep longing. Know yourself, and be comfortable with you. When you are comfortable with you, devoid of arrogance but full of confidence, then you can truly appreciate the life that surrounds you.

"Know thyself, and love what you know. Then not only can your heart breathe, it can soar fueled with unflappable joy!"

—JAPHY TINYSPEAR

AMERICA

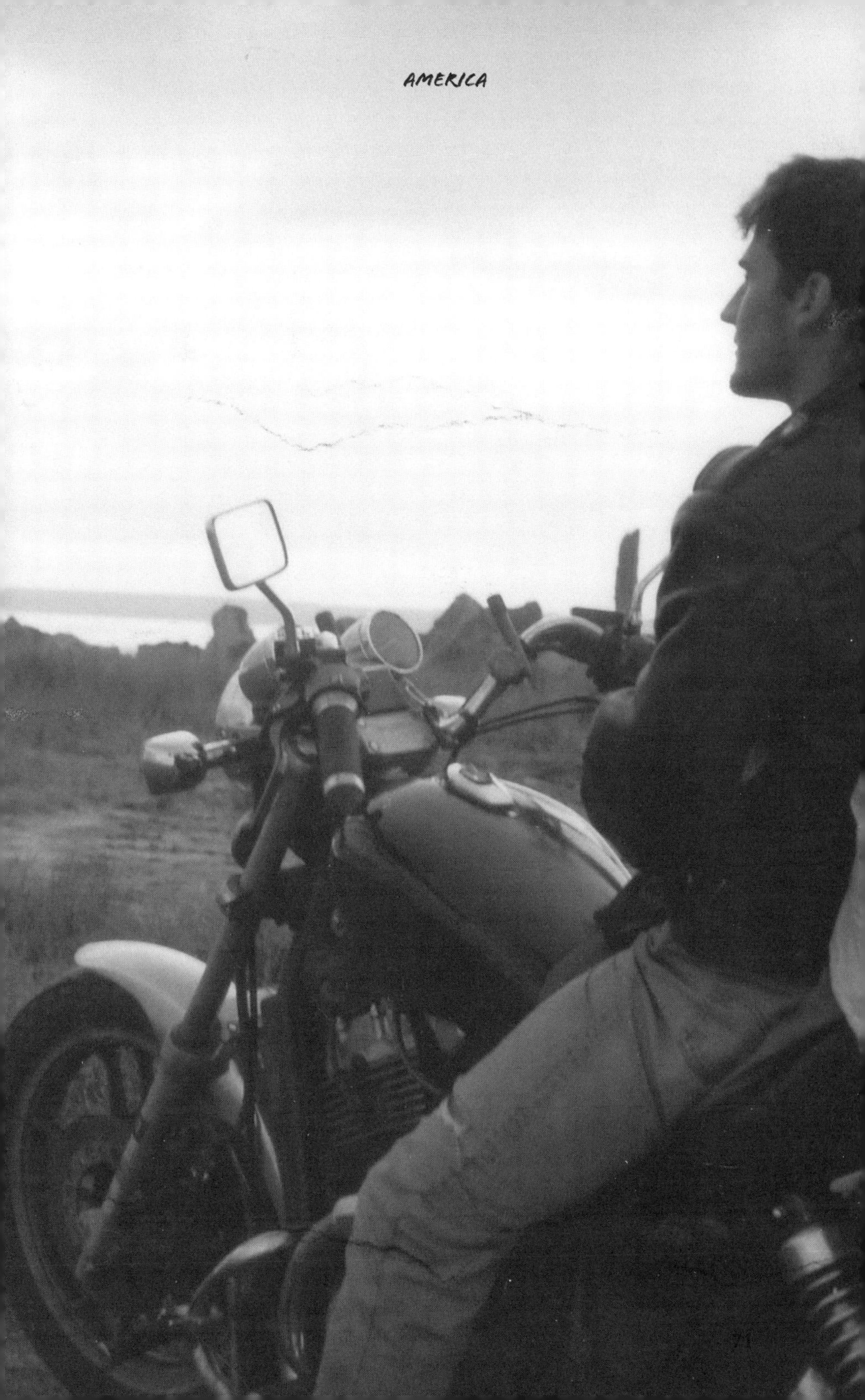

"Is this the dirt road,
Winding through windy trees,
That I must travel?"

—RICHARD WRIGHT,
This Other World, written somewhere in France

PILGRIMAGE
THREE
BRITISH ISLES

APRIL 22
Brighton, England

Today I arrived in Gatwick Airport, U.K., and hitchhiked down to Brighton (it's a Quadrephenia thing). Right now I'm sitting in a pub near the beach enjoying a pint of Guinness. I met two absolutely brilliant chemists from Oxford on the flight over, and they tried to teach me how to make homemade beer (which I've already forgotten). I caught a ride through the green and rolling hills of southern England from a man with a huge heart who willingly shared his life story with me. The sun is shining (but last week they had snow), and the sights, sounds, and smells are overwhelming.

There is another side to this picture, the cloud to this silver lining. Everything is over double the price it ought to be. It took me twice as long to hitch a ride as memory teased, and my pack was heavier than even the worst memory spoke of. And despite my excitement at finally having arrived, I sure miss a ton of people already. The real smacks hard against the ideal, and today smarts.

As soon as I finish my pint, I plan to take out my guitar and strum a little welcome tune. It's the least I can do.

Before I hopped on the plane, my brother Mark asked me what my way, my philosophy was. "What is the Tao of How?" he asked. This summer is my attempt at clarifying an answer to myself, and then perhaps articulating one to him. Perhaps the Tao cannot be articulated, and Socrates, and Lao Tzu all knew this, and cringe at any self-defeating attempt to do so. Even Jesus says, "I AM the truth," and not, "I point to the truth." Nevertheless, this summer I intend to live and think and be; and perhaps the result will be something tangible, perhaps not. The attempt alone means ARETE, the Greek concept of excellence, of fulfilling purpose. Contemplation. Silence. My eyes will be open to wonder.

It's going to be a good summer.

Sage gave me this journal. It is leather bound and beautiful, art already. She asked me to write her a bestseller, but I don't think I can do it. I can, however, choose a theme. It is this: LOVE. Just love. I don't care how expensive things are, or how the rain sucks, or about anything else that might be seen as contradictory to my theme. With every breath I take, I am aware of love. My belly feels it; there are flutters and movements that cannot be attributed to airplane food. There may not always be a smile on my face, but there is one upon my soul, and this is the key to traveling in this fallen world. The other key is a good pen/paper combo, and thankfully, it seems I've got both.

APRIL 23
Hayward's Heath, England

I left Brighton and hitched a ride to Hayward's Heath. It is a quaint little town, and after exploring it, I realized that it did not offer any sort of lodging whatsoever. So I hoofed it two miles to a town even more quaint: Cuckfield, which simply oozed with time and cobblestone. I spoke with a lady at a bed & breakfast there (begging for a free room, but not a chance), and she recommended the Anchorhold Inn, which she said sometimes accepts traveling wilburys like me for a few odd jobs rather than cash. But it was located two miles back in Hayward's Heath, and since I was hungry for countryside and adventure, I kept walking. About seven miles later, I am seriously questioning my sanity. I enter a town called Billingshurst. I buy a cold drink from a store there and eat some leftover bread from my pack, and realize that there is no more stroll left in me.

"There is a time for being ahead,
a time for being behind;
a time for being in motion,
a time for being at rest;
a time for being vigorous,
a time for being exhausted;
a time for being safe,
a time for being in danger.
The Master sees things as they are,
And does not try to control them."

—Tao De Ching, Canto 29

The chalkboard I carry still says Hayward's Heath, and the
Anchorhold Inn sounds wonderful, so I thumb a ride from two
giggling young English women (when I said "hi," they giggled, and
continued for the entirety of our ride) who drop me off at the front
walk. The Anchorhold Inn is not really an inn, but a quiet estate
upon a shady hillside. It consists of a manor hall, a workhouse, and
a few cottages. I explain my situation to the apparent master of the
manor, and he says he can put me up in the workhouse. I follow him,
expecting to be sleeping on the floor with the sawdust and the odd
socket wrench. However, in the rear of the workshop, a bedroom is
hidden, a lovely thing that includes a heater, the softest bed imaginable,
and a bathroom. The master, who reminds me of Sonny Salsbury, the
Ghormley Meadow Camp director, suggests that instead of paying
anything, I just tidy up and sweep in the morning. This is not a
problem.

Today I sat on the main street of Hayward's Heath and played guitar
for a good hour. Not a pence. No one stopped to listen; no one made
eye contact with me. People walked across the street to avoid the
obligation, it seemed. I must have sucked. But I'm not discouraged. A
lady yelled at me from her car, "You won't see any polly around here,
mate!" I yelled back, "It's a good thing I enjoy this"; she smiled and
said, "Cheers."

I gave two people the peace sign today, and then I remembered that
it means the finger here. Sorry.

It is full daylight and past 7:30 p.m., and I am in a nearby pub
having supper and a Tennent's Extra. The barmaid's name is Nikki,
and she smiles at me. I am invited to breakfast at the manor tomorrow
morning, but I must knock upon the door no earlier than 7:15, and
no later than 7:25. Since I don't have a watch, this exactness concerns
me.

Today life is like a long, hard walk. You can quit anytime, but
everyone knows that quitting is sissy, and besides, the scenery just gets
better and better. Also, when you do happen to get tired, with your
feet and your back hurting, it's best to sit down on a patch of grass,
play the guitar, and sing. Rejuvenate. Revitalize. Enjoy a draught of ice
water. And you're on your way again.

The smile is an action that can always be performed; it tends to create the emotions that some think must precede it. My smile started in the first shared moment of my parents; it won't end before the laughter of my grandson's grandson.

A last note: The quote at the beginning of today's entry is from the twenty-ninth canto of the Tao. I am amazed at how very much it resembles Ecclesiastes. "To everything, turn, turn, turn." I'm not suggesting plagiarism; I'm just thinking that the same spirit underlies both.

I suppose it's only fair to note that the barmaid has effectively avoided me for the entirety of my residence here, save for the smile. I am currently taking a great deal of joy listening to the two philosophers at the bar. They're English. Even village idiots sound intelligent.

APRIL 24
Hayward's Heath, England

The nice lady at the bed & breakfast warned me that they were a bit "ecclesiastical." Perhaps she debated on using the word "monastery," but decided in favor of a less medieval description. So I had been warned.

After awakening from a toasty cozy sleep, I jog to where I can spot the clock tower in order to determine my relation to the 7:15 knocking/breakfast time. From afar, the clock informs my sleepy eyes that 7:30 is ten minutes gone. My "better late than never" attitude (as well as the prospect of a free breakfast) convinces me to run to the master with an apology for my tardiness. I'm kicking myself for my

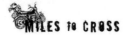

insensitivity to his specific time request for my arrival. Out of breath
and wavering in resolution, I pull on the bell. One of the colleagues
opens the door and informs me in a whisper that it is 6:40 a.m.,
and that everyone within is participating in "services." I apologize
as fervently as possible and then retire to my room to wait for my
embarrassment to subside. Forty minutes later, I knock on the door
and ask for a broom to clean with, and the master motions for me
to enter. He leads me through the long mahogany hallways until we
reach the breakfast room. Things are feeling a bit surreal.

In the center of the room is a huge wooden table; around the table
sit twelve or so men. At the head of the table sits a man so old I think
he might disintegrate, wearing long flowing black robes. The master
(or at least the man I initially thought was the master) whispers,
"Father, a guest," by means of introduction, and I step forward to shake
his hand, partially fearful that I'll crush it into powder. The master
(or the man previously referred to as the master, having immediately
changed my mind due to meeting the ancient frail one) motions to
the table and breathes to me, "Cereal, toast." Then he exits.

I look timidly around. Every eye looks directly to plate;
all concentration is directed toward a methodical manner of
consumption. Silence reigns. I sit and begin to work on a bowl of
cornflake substitute. Every bite I take thunders around the room.
For a few moments, silence beats upon my head. The old quivering
man slowly heaves himself to his feet, and shuffles out. Then, one
by one, each man grabs his plate and leaves. Nobody says a word.
And suddenly I'm sitting alone at a huge table, and for the first time
I realize that the warmth on my lower body is being supplied by
the breath of large, friendly black lab whom I call Rex. I give Rex
a nibble of toast and a head scratch, but Rex remains subdued, a
manifestation of his master's silence. Upon the walls of this room
are pictures of Saints, and of Mary, and there also appeared to be
small statures of Buddha and perhaps Vishnu. As soon as my tea was
suitably cool, I pounded it and bailed. I'm not saying I was freaked
out, but I was a bit freaked out. As I was leaving, the master (the
original one, not the powdery old one) arrived with a broom, and a
handshake. He said, "Good luck with your travels and all," and then he
did an absolutely delightful thing. He smiled. That knocked me flat.

Whenever I feel I've got things figured out, life throws an upper cut that floors me.

It's still early, and I've just finished a Danish at a small coffee shop in the town center. I have no real plans for the day. I hope it doesn't rain.

Later: It is night on the same day, and I'm in a London youth hostel listening to Queen's "Bohemian Rhapsody." I can't remember ever being as lonely as I am right now. It's kind of cool. Sometimes when I get lonely, my soul sort of revels in it, especially when it's a non-descriptive type of loneliness that just leaves me longing for everything. Earlier I walked through Hyde Park in the rain, listening to *Phantom of the Opera*, and I almost wept like a ninny.

So here I am in the most beautiful city in the world, and clouds hang above my head and in my heavy heart. I can only hope for union with those I love in my dreams. How is it possible to desire freedom so badly it destroys you? Or maybe freedom is what I have, and it's destroying me. How is it that I never guessed traveling alone in England I would be so alone?

APRIL 25
London

The wind blows marshmallow puff clouds across a deep blue sky. I'm sitting on the bank of a river that runs through Hyde Park, and

appreciating a pair of geese feeding just in front of me. Yesterday I walked to 56 Princes Gate to see my residence for the summer. Oh nice. Oh very nice. It appears to be placed in the middle of the cultural arts center of London. Museums on both sides, the Imperial College just across the street, with the Royal Albert Hall down the way. Hyde Park is literally next-door.

My first introduction to Hyde Park comes from Douglas Adams in *So Long and Thanks for All the Fish*. He describes it on a summer afternoon, and writes that it is impossible not to be in love when you're here. As I look around, I see couples holding hands, holding each other, and loving like mad. I am the Chronicler who watches, feels, and loves, but the object of my affection is life ... which is slightly non-tangible, difficult to hug.

My face is shaven; my clothes are clean. Mothers are no longer pulling their children away from me whispering, "Honey, don't bother that man." I have been sitting here for quite a while. I think I shall go to Portabello Road.

APRIL 27
London

    This is to be my last night in this hostel, and I am, to say the least, looking forward to leaving. Actually, as hostels go, this one is fairly nice, and the travelers here are interesting, but I am tired of the money it takes to stay here. I've been hanging with Australians who are looking for work, and they are filled with exuberance. I get a charge just hanging around them. We heard that the guy working the counter at our hostel was the local weed supplier, but last night our hostel was raided by the police, and I don't think he'll be supplying locally for a while.

I've bought and read *The Hobbit*. It is continually a masterpiece. I miss my Tolkien/Monday Night Football buddy Alex.

Last night I dreamed. The lady I miss came to me and took my hand, and I was wooed. She lead me to a chair, sat me down, and kneeled in front of me, clasping my legs. She turned her face to one side, laid her head in my lap, and explained very carefully that we would never be together. Then she laughed, and I sobbed awake with a lump in my throat. I can only hope that this was no revelation of future events, but a night demon having his way with me. I'm glad to be awake. It would be nice to keep this type of rejection to my waking life.

Life might be like a subway ride. Strictly utilitarian, and the view is dark. Some, however, choose to climb off of the subway, to walk with sky overhead and grass underfoot. Up until this point in my life, sunshine and breeze take priority. I hope they always will.

"Knowing others is intelligence;
Knowing yourself is true wisdom.
Mastering others is strength;
Mastering yourself is true power."
—Tao

APRIL 30
London

Today the world is gray, but sunshine and laughter hold court in my heart. My room with a view is cozy and already like home. I was up early today for a shower and call to the folks before breakfast. Then I sat on the huge stairs leading up from the ground floor with Teresa and Wiles (we are in the same program) for quality conversation before a guitar session in front of millions of roaring imaginary fans. It has been a good morning. No classes today, so an easy mellowness prevails. My nose drips London quietly. I saw a falcon strike today. I was virtually alone in the rain, walking through Hyde Park, when I noticed an enormous flock of pigeons huddling on the ground, attempting to stay dry. Suddenly, every bird on the ground took to flight. I was right in their midst, and quite startled as hundreds of birds ascended instantly. Immediately to my right I saw a reddish-blur swoop lightning fast, and then it rose, much slower, with a dead pigeon in its talons. This city has everything! I tried to keep my eyes open the rest of the day.

Musings: The Tao is too much "accept the world as it is," and Christianity seems too much "change and save the world." "The Tao that can be told is not the eternal Tao," seems to reverberate down into Paul Tillich's, "God must be a symbol for God." Tillich, a Christian Existentialist, also feels that each generation must redefine its own symbol of the divine in order for faith to be alive and not mere idolatry. He is a Christian who feels that the Bible is a period-potent symbolization of the divine, but is rooted too heavily in the past to provide an ultimate concern for those of this century. Through the realization that it is a symbol, the Bible can then be adapted into something that is more potent in this existential world. It's his answer

as to how I can see a dusty desert book as the tome that contains the deepest yearnings of my heart. However, I wonder if the problem is in applying this book to my life. It might only work to apply my life to this book.

The Tao, on the other hand, seems to realize this from the start. By its very structure, it speaks in ambiguities, and in doing so, lends timelessness to its poetry. Yet, I do feel that the sentiment is too much "the world is sacred; you can't improve or change it." I believe positive and negative change is possible with every action, every word spoken, every smile, and every curse.

On the other side again, I feel Christianity wants too much change. Kierkegaard realized that when you create a Christian kingdom, what happens is that the kingdom ceases to be Christian in that instant. He is right, of course. Nobody wants a world of Pharisees. Calvin's Geneva was anything but paradise. Only with The Return of the King (Tolkien imagery, of course) can any sort of paradise be imagined. Still, kingdom building in preparation of the King's return whispers of significance to my conflicted, shallow soul.

Which reveals another truth I discover I'm holding: I do believe the sandal-clad Christ from Nazareth is the incarnation of the divine. I think I'm discovering that I've believed it for some time. And, like Kierkegaard, I realize that the only way I can "know" this is through a leap of faith, something that transcends both the ethical and the rational. I also believe that many of the things Jesus said and did were done with a great deal of Zen. He spoke in parables and ambiguities, and the truth was brought in such a way that each individual was forced to discover it on their own (Socrates did this as well, but much more aggressively). So I agree with the masses. Jesus WAS a great teacher. And maybe, just maybe, because I do believe He was a great teacher, I can believe what He taught about Himself. Maybe.

Screw it. Yes. YES. I might as well be honest, I believe; I've thrown my lot in with HIM; I've chosen a side. There is no way I can claim to have the answers ... Like Jacob, perhaps, I'm still wrestling with God on many fronts. But I'm in. I'm IN. And it feels good to know. I'm in. Jesus, I'm in. Interesting to me how I got here. No altar calls. No high pressure sales. Like Van Morrison says, "no guru, no method, no teacher. Just you and I and nature, in the garden, wet with rain."

up early
before the sun
reading emerson, tao, lewis, matthew
and waking up, bit by bit,
      the thing that
            sleeps within soul

while reading
and thinking and scratching
      notes on various
            paper products
      my heart is lifted up
blood pulsing at my temples
      my eyes raise from
            the half-glaze
                  open
            fully alert
light breaks over the mountains
      through the window
            flooding the loft where I sit
                  blinding,
      yet illuminating
            warmly wrapping me
                  emerson

*I think to myself
this is a glimpse of what
joy must be like
zen-peaceful
filled with love and God
ready for journey, possibility,
anything at all
then again,
perhaps it's just the coffee.*

These are thoughts I have as I study and live and become. The Tao of How dictates that I continue to explore, think, appreciate, and wonder. But at least I know I'm in. For now, London is calling, and my duty seems to be to answer her with sweater and smile.

MAY 2
London

Received notes from loved ones today, and have these thoughts: We all shine on (thank you, Instant Karma) ... the world is tiny, and each member vitally important, yet sometimes it feels as if no connections are made, and each one a star in the night separated by vast gulfs in the darkness. Today dawned cold and wet after a terrifying dream that death beckoned to me from the corner of my room, and I was struck with the post-fear realization that life is like a prize that kids send cereal box tops in for, with the entirety of it spent in hopeful anticipation of the arrival of Something Wonderful, and finally, the dream is not so much realized, but merely ended, and disappointment reigns.

So, a lump in my throat for no reason, and I feel alone and motivated to do nothing at all. Independence is a thing I prize, but today, and many times, it seems a curse I have cast upon myself. I miss ... to begin a list would take a greater part of this next week, so suffice it to say that I miss the things I love. People, weather, ideals, my dog ... everything except for the two things I have. I have my own life, and right now the independence I treasure is larger than I am and laughing at me. I also have the love of somebody special; or at least I think I do, and the mere hope wars with my loneliness and will emerge victorious.

MAY 3
London

I am sitting amid the meticulously manicured beauty of Kensington Gardens, and the surrounding beauty combined with the love songs in my Walkman provide a sort of in-body firework show. Cyndi has sent me a tape, and it touches me. There are many people out, for it is a fine Sunday afternoon, yet I am seated within a peaceful alcove surrounded on three sides by flowers and trees. I was told today that Sir Barrie walked in these gardens with several neighborhood children and told them stories of an amazing, flying, playing, crowing boy-faun with the classical title Pan. It is easy to imagine. Peter's statue stands near the lake.

An elderly lady has seated herself on the bench next to me and is feeding the squirrels and sparrows that laugh here. I gave her a small smile, but no response, so I leave the Walkman on; we remain separate and unconnected. Great numbers of pigeons have joined us and feed and coo merrily. Yet each one pushes and fights to gorge itself on the tastiest morsels, and it seems that they reflect society, in a Jonathon Livingston Seagull sort of way. One sparrow with a bright orange breast flits and hops about for fun, apparently. He lights on the bench and cocks his head to look at me, then chirps twice before bolting on to more amusing pursuits.

There is a glory that this day speaks of, and it isn't mine. My praise

is becoming much more personal, my gratitude a personal gratitude. God, You are good. Please open my eyes to see Your goodness where it may be found.

MAY 6
Leominster, England

I glance across the floor of this room to a dusty chalkboard that says Leominster. It's the fourth name that has appeared on the board today. Oxford, Cheltenham, and Ross-on-Wye preceded it. Five rides today, and I'm halfway to the northern coast of Wales, which is my destination. The man who drove me to Cheltenham was named David, married to Meg, with an adorable pug named Bonny. I know, because he took me to his house for tea and an egg and potatoes. We shared delightful conversation about education and the justice system (once again, fabricating a working knowledge of topics I knew nothing about); then he dropped me off at a prime thumb location and tooted his horn as he drove away. I waved with big smile, and I meant it. Then five minutes later I was flying over green hillsides in a convertible piloted by two university men. They took me past Ross-on-Wye, which was the town on my board, to Hereford, which was the place I was making for anyway. A mayfair was there, with carnival lights spinning, and tonight I felt them brash and out of place on the majestic trophy of culture that makes up England. So I picked the next town, Leominster, to adorn my slate, and Nick provided the transport. We began with small chat, and practically before we had exchanged names, he had offered me his flat as a bedding site. As it was past 9 p.m. and dark, I accepted. So I spent some time with him and his roommates, and then prepared my bed.

I am tired ... much too tired for mental musings. But I must make an observation. As a hitchhiker, I see a few standard responses to my sign. The best response (short of a ride) is any sort of communication; for example, sympathetic gestures from the driver indicating he would like to stop but can't just now, etc. The next best response is when the driver curiously looks at the sign and makes positive eye contact. This shows that the person is wide-eyed and examining the world about, keeping possibilities and options open. On more than one occasion,

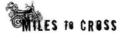

I've seen the instant dreaminess hit of a longing for new roads, new ways, and no agenda. Do it, friend! When the wanderlust hits, proceed! The poorest sort are those who see me from afar yet avoid looking at my slate or myself as they pass. It seems to me that these people are rigid—that their lives consist of various well-defined roles, and hitchhikers on Wednesday afternoons don't fit the script. Possibilities, options, and a great deal of life are unavailable because of a choice to be closed. I pity them, and vow to remain a free man. Sleep masters me without resistance, and for a time I fade.

Impatience is the
great laugh.
It is choosing mirage
while stumbling past
oasis
after
oasis
Life is what happens
in the meantime

MAY 7
Leominster, England

    Up bright (sort of) and early, and off to the nearest bakery for toast and coffee. The toast was rather predictable, but the coffee quite brilliant. My cup was empty much too quickly. Several elderly ladies are about, and their chatter and obvious friendship warms this traveler. This morning, life is very hopeful, and a faith in humanity and goodness comes without effort. Nature, and the splendor of the rolling countryside, only increase my enthusiasm. I'm quite wired on life, actually. And I'm very hopeful about another cup of coffee.

a beam of sun traveling
distances
Ignoring clouds
filling valleys
climbing mountaintops
illuminating things hidden
flooding dark corners of shade
weaving through rooftops
even finding space between
thick curtain and windowsill
to bind me
as I sit
sipping my coffee

MAY 8
Llanderis, Wales

Last night I pampered myself and checked into a quaint little bed & breakfast in the walled township of Cowry on the northern coast of Wales. Rides were a blessing yesterday, and Rhoda, a bustling mother figure, took me a great distance along my road and showed me her house, where we shared a pot of tea. Already I've seen several castles, but yesterday I climbed all over a magnificent fighting structure built by Edward I to subdue the Welsh revolutionaries.

Today, who knows? "You never know your luck ... That's what I like about life," says a burley lorry driver who advanced my journey yesterday. And he is right. You never do.

I'm finishing up a breakfast with great coffee and small talk with Tom and his wife from Liverpool. They sound like The Beatles.

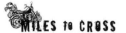

There are some high rocky hills behind the house that afford an excellent view of the coastline. Last night at dusk I climbed them, and the wind at the top was like a gale, and I was afraid. But I staggered, as if under a burden, to the very northern edge, which was sheer, and sat. The wind ravaged my body, and I was facing it, and I felt like I was in flight. I flew low along the green hillsides of the coast, out past the Isle of Angsley, and, gathering speed, headed west toward a glorious sunset. I opened my eyes, and a gull was motionless in the air beside me, hovering, still, with the wind streaming over the two of us. Then he gently dipped down to the left, and with no perceptible movement of his wings, rose rapidly to the right, higher and higher, and north. In an instant, the gull was gone. I was dizzy, amazed, afraid, and thrilled. My soul laughed in relish; I was drunk without beverage. It's impossible to describe, but it was so beautiful and so surreal, Dali and Disney; fantasy.

Today, I climb a mountain.

End of the day. I walked a lot today—more than eight miles with my pack. It began when the nice lady from the bed & breakfast gave me directions to the highway I needed. "Don't go out by the main road, dear," she said in a delightful brogue, "there's nothing to see. Go to the left, here, and follow the road 'round, and you'll come to it." And I did come to it, after about five miles of glorious rain-drenched countryside passed under my boot. I say "rain drenched," for the rain was indeed drenching. I loved it, the walk and the rain. "Adventures are not always may-walks in sunshine," Mr. Baggins was fond of saying. "Never laugh at live dragons" was another of his proverbs. A live dragon might have helped warm my soggy bum.

It rains
the windows are bleary,
   tear stained
the hills through the window
   withdraw quiet
    shattered
like shades of green in a kaleidoscope
  connecting not with the real
    It rains.

   soft on the roof
footsteps of angels, perhaps, or elves
  dancing catlike on the house,
  slow now, then faster
to some unsung tune they dance
  making merry, or melancholy
    It rains.

the fields beyond being pushed,
    pulled,
    parted,
  this way and that,
  frantic by the wind
    going nowhere
   It rains.

I did not climb a mountain today, but I was near the top of one. The Penn-y-Pass youth hostel is located at a height, and is the only pass through this part of the mountains that make up Snowdownia. I was supposed to meet my friends at the hostel there, but I failed to do so because I was early. The hostel is closed from 10 a.m. to 5 p.m. every day, and I arrived at noon. So I left a note for Troy and Kelly (a mad fisherman from Alaska, and a poet in the sense of embodiment—he and Troy are also in my program. Or, I'm in theirs) and thumbed a ride to a town that was lower down (but not warmer).

I'm in a hostel now, but I almost spent the night in the ruins of a castle. I hiked about two miles out of town (Llanderis, I think) to a completely untended castle. It was mysterious and moss-covered, and although most of it was foundation walls, one large tower was completely intact. Unfortunately, it was open to the sky, and therefore everything was wet. One stairwell that let to the top was relatively dry, but it was small and steep and offered no rest to this weary traveler. But my goal is to spend the night in a ruin, on a fine night with a fire, and perhaps an elf or two.

It's getting dark. The lights of the town are appearing and look eerie in the fog. This hostel is built on a hill that overlooks the town and valley and the river that creeps through it. I can hear sheep bleating. It is cold. My supper of baked beans and bread settles nicely into my body; I've treated myself to an orange for dessert.

Tonight life is like a fog covered-mountain ... beauty, glory, and majesty, together with mystery. Impressive, impassive, and you can never quite see all of it.

Or maybe that is an analogy of God. And the more you see, the smaller you become. But it's a good thing.

MAY 9
Caenarfon, Wales

I'm sitting in a café that looks out across the street to the Caenarfon Castle. Another impregnable fighting structure.

The coffee here is superb. It is freezing outside. This morning I caught a lift back up to the hostel at Penn-y-Pass to meet Troy and Kelly from Pepperdine. There was a note for me saying that they had left at 10 a.m. to go hiking, and as it was 5 minutes to 10 a.m., I figured I just missed them. It was sheeting a freezing rain, and I had no desire to go hiking in it anyway. So I left a note and bolted for a more coastal climate (which in Wales also means a sheeting, freezing rain).

Love.

I wrote Love to remind myself of the first law of my life. And to bring to mind the very second law, which is, "No complaints."

I'm fairly thawed now, and the castle begs me to explore. I just belched a little too loudly to be in public. All in all, it's a good day.

MAY 10
London

Tired, happy, and home. A long day of hitching and hiking to bring me to London from Portmadog, Wales, where I spent the night. The two workers who drove me to Portmadog invited me to join them for a pint to watch the biggest football match of the year: the English Cup Final. We had a blast. We got snookered. It was a good time, that ended with me just crashing on their couch. The day began with a mouth of desert-dry cotton, begging through parched lips and migraine, "Water, water."

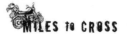

It's been a full day of return hitching and great conversation with my drivers. I'm home, exhausted, clean, and on my way to bed. A glance up at the half moon, a smile, and my soul is glad.

Liverpool won the cup.

MAY 12
London

Sunset in London. The Dome tower of Imperial College becomes luminescent once more. I write by candlelight. There are two oranges on my desk among the various books and odd ends that are scattered there. The one on the right begs to be eaten.

When the sun sets, the sky gathers the most incredible shades of blue. It is clear tonight, and the first star of the evening smiles down, twinkling merrily upon this candlelit student. Tonight I am full of emotion, but a good, pinnacle of life kind of thing, and I revel in my solitude. Maybe later I will grab a pint with Shana or someone else from our house. Right now I am content. Mellow tunes waft my soul to the Ethereal. And I'm packing my bags for the Misty Mountains.

Apparently I haven't much to say. Life seems very pleasing to me. Thanks, Lord. Lord Jesus. Kyrie Iesu Xristo. I read a verse this week, Romans 10:9, which says "… if thou shalt confess with thy mouth the Lord Jesus, and shalt believe in thine heart that God hath raised him from the dead, thou shalt be saved." I believe. This is my confession. Lord I believe, help thou my unbelief. Being saved doesn't feel like I thought it would. It feels clean. I feel clean. Now when I look in the mirror, I can imagine what peace is, and the imaginings are good. I have never understood what having Jesus in my heart meant; I still don't. But I know what it means to have Him in my life. He is closer to me than my own mind. And His thoughts toward me are all GOOD. I still haven't been to a church service. I've visited a myriad of cathedrals, and I'll hunt my way through a myriad more. Cathedrals aren't the pilgrimage, but they point to it. Monuments to glory, designed to house majesty, they instead merely hint skyward … inviting pilgrims to take another step, and another, and yet one more, into the presence of God.

I don't believe in relics. A leg bone of a saint, fingernails housed in a holy trinket … I reject the magic charm philosophy. But I believe in the faith of those who have become relics. Once vibrant and alive, at one time giants of humility, these men and women walked daily in the presence of God. Now they are entombed, dry, brittle, and lifeless. The relics are a symbol of the Christian faith itself. Christianity as an institution has become dry and brittle. Europe has walked away. America is walking. Oh, Jesus! Oh Holy Fire! Ignite these relics! Incarnate these bones! Make what has become lifeless full of Your life! Animate what once brought You glory, so that You might receive rightful glory again. Jesus, not faith as an institution. But Lord, ignite the faith as a powerful relationship of love. Allow this fallen place to see that what its heart greedily clamors for can ultimately only be satisfied in You.

And Jesus, thank You. You have awed this member of creation into a quiet soul-smile, and I can only shine eyes in gratitude. The stars are singing softly to one another, the song is ancient, small, and clear. It is the Song, and tonight, I join. Thanks for the invitation.

MAY 14
London

It is an absolutely beautiful sunshine day, and I am lying in
Kensington Gardens listening to Van Morrison. Van Morrison is on
my mind today because his daughter is the lovely Shana mentioned
previously. We are both travelling to Bath this weekend, which is
where the man the Van lives. Perhaps I shall meet him, perhaps not.
Nonetheless, Van Morrison and the sun stone me to my soul, and it is
good. I saw *Les Miserables* last night. Of course it made me ache with a
passion for selfless glory, and I wanted to destroy the rude tourists who
were tittering throughout. I think I'll nap.

MAY 16
Bath, England

Canterbury yesterday and a trip down the Pilgrims Way. It was
delightful and touristy, and I enjoyed myself. I was sampling a pint
and began a conversation with a lonely man there. I know he was
lonely, for when I prepared to go, he hurriedly offered to buy me a
pint, which I, of course, accepted. Then down to the coast through
Hastings, where a construction worker gave me a lift and offered to
smoke me out with his wife. It was a kind gesture, and I thanked him
for that, but I was on my guard after my pints in Canterbury (I'm
pretty sure Lonely Dude was trying to hit on me), and I wanted to
be in some kind of shape for hitching. Plus, I'm traveling with Christ.
Would He want me lighting up? Somehow that is a picture I can't
see, of Jesus and the disciples, passing the bong around. "When you've
seen me, you've seen the Father," Jesus says, "now Peter, quit bogarting
that joint." Nope. I can see Him turning water into wine. But it's
interesting that there is no hint of debauchery in the account of it.
There was a higher plane of existence on which Christ lived—one
that was selfless, not out to please self, which is the beginning aim of
all drug use. He had a moral perspective that was superior (in a literal
sense of the word), and that always saw the highest purpose possible
in any situation. I wrote Toph a letter this week and told him that I
get it now. Being a follower of Jesus is a seven-day-a-week, twenty-

four-hour-a-day thing. Kelly showed me a quote from C.S. Lewis which said, "If Christianity is true, then it is of infinite importance. If false, then of no importance. One thing it cannot be is of moderate importance." He's right. And it's time for me to take it up a notch.

On through Eastbourne, where I spent the night on a hilltop field with an otherworldly view of ocean and moon. Today rides in plenty, and now at 2 p.m., I find myself in Bath. I'm having a salad and gathering change to call Shana. I hope she's in.

MAY 17
En route to London from Stonehenge

She was. We spent a delightful evening talking and laughing and quaffing pints of ale. I spoke briefly to Van Morrison on the phone. He said, "Hello?" and I asked, "Is Shana in?" He said, "Yeah, hold on a sec." So I can say from experience he seems like a normal guy. As Shana and I were talking, she asked me several questions about my travels. She seemed interested in where I would stay that night, and I was hoping to get an invitation to stay over at her dad's. So I truthfully answered that I was just sleeping outside in a field. Unfortunately, she seemed to love the vagabond idea of me staying out in a field, wandering around the country, and so she offered me nothing. As I was not bold enough to do more than hint, I really can't blame her. "You are on an adventure!" She said, delighted. "It's a lost art!" I didn't have the balls to go into how much greater an adventure it would be to sleep on the floor in Van Morrison's garage. The fainthearted can get this near to legend, but no nearer. I'm not bitter. This isn't bitterness.

"You never know your luck." I heard that again as Cod (great name) dropped me off at the ancient mystics gathering place, which he described as a pile of rocks. Stonehenge is majestic, magical, and it reeks of the supernatural. But it is also a tourist attraction, and on this Sunday, hundreds mill about gazing at this attraction from a respectable distance (due to the ropes, I'm sure). The distance from which I gaze is slightly more respectable, for I refuse to pay the admission fee. Today it is slightly against my principles, but more pragmatically opposed to my budget, which at this stage is non-existent.

Last night as I slept outside (despite my hint-dropping evening with Shana), an interesting scene unfolded. I was sleeping in a farmer's field just outside of Bath when someone blundered through the trees and almost stepped on me. I cried out, and the guy ran back to the trees and disappeared, but I could tell he just stopped in the shadows. There was no answer when I asked who he was, just more rustling. So I packed up my stuff and headed off to find a more secure resting place. I ended up in somebody's garden, but it was so late the foxes were out (I saw two), and I didn't disturb a soul.

I forgot to mention that the night before last I heard witches. It was a full moon, and I was in an isolated field on a hillside (outside of Eastbourne). The field was bordered by trees, and the grass was close to three feet high. At one point, I was suddenly awakened by a loud female cackle and laughter at the top of the hill behind the trees. It grew in volume for half a moment or so—then silence. Seconds later, loud cackles sounded from the bottom of the field, again behind the trees. These continued a moment and ceased as abruptly. I suppose it was some sort of broomstick race under the full moon, but perhaps it was just a gaggle of spinsters having fun with a sleeping trespasser.

You never know your luck.

MAY 21
Leeds, England

It is deep dusk, and I am in a field by a river in a little town in the Peak District near Leeds. I'm on my way to Glasgow. Today I had a huge discussion with Kelly about life and truth and belief. I don't know all the answers. I don't. Can one person really know? Can there be certainty despite confusion? But I do know God, and because of HIM:

> I say life's for living.
> Road's for traveling.
> Eye's for wondering.
> Soul's for soaring.
> Bag's for sleeping.
> Heart's for loving.

God, please don't allow me too much success and ease as the devil's advocate. Please don't allow my love of ale and travel disqualify me from a role in Your delight. Do I really have to become a safe, boring Christian in order to love You? Tell me what my heart longs to hear ... that following YOU well is the only true adventure left.

It is getting dark, and I have no light by which to write. I'll lie down and look up and listen. I'll fall asleep thinking of those I love.

This field is full of flowers.

MAY 22
Windermere, England (Lake District)

Vaguely dissatisfied with myself and this day. I've been hiking and hitching since around 8 this morning. It's late afternoon, and only sixty miles or so have passed under my heels. I can't shake the feeling that I'm doing something wrong. Now I'm resting in a little coffee shop. The day is hot but cloudy, and there is no wind. As my body rests, my mood lifts.

The day began well. A lorry driver named Ted drove me to the slip road onto the motorway, assuring me I would have no trouble getting a ride. Fifty minutes later, the same Ted picked me up again. He had made his delivery and felt responsible for me, so he drove me half an hour out of his way to a service station. Ted was a round, red-faced, jolly man, and I was reminded of Tom Bombadil who helped traveling Hobbits twice out of trouble. One ride I had today dropped me in the middle of the motorway, and two different bobbies assured me that my presence on the motorway was illegal. I'm on the back roads again, but so far, not a great deal more luck.

The high point of the day involves Tolkien; I finished reading
The Lord of the Rings again. Without question, my enjoyment of this
reading surpasses even the first Tolkien experience I've had. The laws
of diminishing returns have no claim on the man. Once again I was
amazed, moved, and left smiling, with a lump in my throat and a song
in my heart. Oh, to live in the Shire in 1420 (Shire Reckoning) ... to
laugh and ride with Merry and Pippin ... to be full of wonder and sail
quietly over the sea with Frodo and Gandalf and Galadriel! Middle
Earth is too full, to large, too real in my thought to be non-existent.
Someday perhaps, in a world where imagination and reality become
one, Aragorn, Gandalf, and Tolkien himself will clad me in chain mail
and lead me through the world that we know. Probably not. If this is
as good as it gets, it's enough.

The afternoon wanes, and I must attempt to move northward. There
is a music festival in Glasgow on Sunday, with Van Morrison playing
and Shana sneaking me in ... if I can get there, that is.

Night. You never know your luck, they say, and like most simple
sayings, it's true. Three rides later with a waiting time of, oh, say
four minutes total, I find myself upon the outskirts of Glasgow. I'm
grinning, tapping my fingertips together, and muttering "excellent"
with great gusto.

I've just finished a meal of bread, beans, raisins, coffee, and water.
My insides thank me with soft murmurs. There are fields outside that
call to me, "Sleep, sleep, sweet, Elysian peace be yours here, with all
warmth and cozy snuggle as well." Only they lie, because it is a chill
moist night, and promises increase in both the chill and moist aspects.
I shall sleep in all manner of clothing.

MAY 24
Glasgow, Scotland

Cold tile under me bum. Cold thoughts in my soul. I have
descended into shadow, and sunshine and laughter are to me a dream.
There is no sun in Glasgow, nor sky; there is only cloud, and cloud
cloaks me and enters me until my very soul is wreathed in gloom.
I am alone, and my vision of fair things is dimmed. Even as the
ring-bearer wanders blind through the darkness of Mordor, so too I

stumble through ugliness, harshness, and dark. The man who isolates himself seeks his own desire, the Proverb says. He rages against all sound judgment, the Proverb warns. The result is a soul in chains, I testify. And here I am in the cloud.

Perhaps I am spreading it on too thick. Or maybe I'm just on the wrong side of town. But the buildings here are huge, dirty, and evil looking. Litter is everywhere. Most of this architecture looks early communist. Last night I stayed in the YMCA, a square building that rose straight into the air over thirty stories. It was hideous. Instead of building flats that hold glimpses of the culture that makes Scotland great, the people of Glasgow have instead opted to construct huge monoliths that obstruct the sky ("I see seven towers, but I only see one way out," Bono says). My eye looks from the filth of the street to the lifeless monstrosities that pass for apartments, from the vacant faces of those riding the buses in silence, to the cheerless cloud; and it's shadow, and these visions cause my soul to blanch.

After verbally vomiting this darkness, I feel better, lighter. Besides, today the Van plays, and if I get in to see him, the cloud will indeed be broken.

I am in Central Station waiting for the arrival of my friends and classmates. I want my hometown; I want family and friends; I want tender caresses and warm sun. I want to surf. I want America. I want good prices for big meals and refills on coffee and coke and iced tea. I want my brother Mark and my brothers of soul, Toph and Alex. I want wholesomeness (meaning that my thoughts have not been), and I want a good tan.

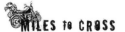
I'm lonely, and the cold tiles have caused my butt to fall asleep. And I have no money. And truly I am the most spoiled of brats. Love.

I suppose somebody likes Glasgow.

MAY 30
London

There is a thunderstorm in the darkness. It rolls and peals and crashes through the sky on this late night; there is no rain. Tonight was laundry and guitar and sit-ups. Loneliness, but the kind that affirms life and creativity. Friends called today.

The last entry was far too pessimistic. And it ended, like most things, in glory and luck. For I met all those designated to be met, and we had a great time boogying to the silky sounds of many Scottish and Irish tunes. Van Morrison, through his daughter, slipped us all VIP guest passes, and that is just about the coolest thing I can think of. Then he jumped onstage and jammed like the crazy mother he is. It was sheer bliss. When he did "Gloria" as his last encore, I thought I was going to burst with joy and shoot my guts all over the place. And finally, late that night, I stowed myself on the overnight train to London without a ticket, and arrived home (unharassed) in time for my 9 a.m. class (which was undoubtedly the most anti-climactic way to end that venture).

This week I make a solo trek to Spain.

JUNE 1
Portbou, Spain

After two day's hard travel, I find myself in a Spanish villa snug within a tiny Mediterranean village nestled within the folds of these Pyrenees Mountains. I am tired, but smiles are springing voluntarily to my lips, rather than being forced like reluctant nap-bound children. I'm pretty close to broke (this room is less than $9 U.S.). France is full of vipers. That might not be true. There are probably only a few greedy, obstinate Frenchmen, and I must have met them all on this trip. The worst was that my train dropped me in Paris at midnight, and my train out didn't leave until 8 the next morning. So I thought I'd just sleep in the station, but they swept us various riff-raff out one by one, and I started looking for a dry place to throw my bag in this city. And then it started raining. So I headed for the hostels that are listed in my *Let's Go*, but they were full, and of course I had no reservations. One of the guys behind the desk recommended a nearby hotel, where he assured me it is cheap. I suppose it is, but it nearly broke me just the same. And when I opened the door to the tiny room I had paid for, the first thing I noticed was that the bed was slightly larger than the broom closet which they sold as a room. The second thing I noticed was that the bed already had two people asleep in it. TWO

men! I'm an American! Does this kind of thing even happen in the world?! By this time, it was creeping on toward 3 a.m., and I thought about going downstairs and crying that if they were going to extort a considerable chunk of my paltry stash of coin, they ought to at least give me the dignity of being bilked in private. But then I thought better of it, and just spooned up next to my faintly snoring bedfellow. Whatever. Adventure sucks sometimes. But I'll tell this one with pride to my grandkids.

This village is called Portbou, and despite the fact that it's 10 p.m. on a Sunday, all the children and townspeople are strolling along the beach or the main boulevard. It is warm. I have hiked about six miles across the border through the mountains, and my private *Sound of Music* soundtrack is blasting through my interior stereo system. The sky is reaching that deep shining blue that sings of eternity. There is an ancient church on the hill that looks sacred and well-visited. It is very beautiful here. I can hear children playing hide-and-seek. My Spanish is very poor, but it has already helped me out with directions and this room. My Catalon is even worse. Love.

Ashley (my Australian sheepdog) calls to me in visions, and we frolic in my dreams.

JUNE 3
L'escala, Spain

L'escala. This long sunset I give to Alex and Toph. On this Mediterranean port of L'escala, I am alone in reality, but united in being with these two friends of soul. For three bucks I have purchased two bottles of Catalonia's finest, and all is slightly humming at this stage. Normally, I disdain drinking alone, pero today I'm with two of my best buds, figuratively speaking, and that just calls for a drink. All the beaches are topless (which is a good thing, because I didn't even think of bringing a top), and (therefore) the scenery is incredible. Toph, Alex, I love you guys, and although I'm dripping with sentimentality, the sunset and sea beg my immediate attention. So, adios, mis compadres, and all peace and joy go with. For myself, a sip, and nostalgia that pierces lonely hearts.

JUNE 4
L'escala, Spain

I just finished a beautiful lunch of tomato sandwiches (homemade in my room with borrowed utensils) and am working myself up for a nice siesta. It is afternoon now, and the day has been spent in the warmth of the Costa Brava sunshine on the beach. Tomorrow I'm heading back toward London, out of cash. I never even made it to Barcelona.

Last night was a great night (my handwriting is difficult to read for some reason), and I wandered all over this gorgeous costal town and watched a sunset that stretched to forever. All was beauty.

I spent a night in Figures, and saw the Dali museum there. The trip begins before you even walk inside the doors. It just may have been the best morning I've ever spent in a museum. The man was playing with a different deck—his visions are alarming and fascinating, and it's obvious he wasn't working with the medium of the normal. I'm so glad.

A quick glance in the mirror shows that I got some sun today. My skin, pale no longer, glares at me in wrath and blaze.

Evening. Outside the sky and clouds are deepest blue, and lightning

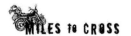

flickers over a sea of glass. It's warm and calm, but it will storm tonight. The night is very beautiful, and my soul thrills to be a part of it.

The family that owns and runs this hotel is gorgeous. I'm in the bar, which is next to the kitchen, which is next to the dining area. The father is the best. He smiles and bubbles continually, and in my mind, he is a good man. There is a daughter as well, quite lovely. Last night I stumbled in with a craving for french fries, and it was quite fun for all as I tried to make myself understood. Oddly enough, the father understood me when I slipped into German and ordered pommes frittes. Today the whole family was big smiles toward me, and I was big smiles back (except mine held bits of embarrassment). I don't exactly know what day it is. I like that.

> "The clouds above us join and separate,
> the breeze in the courtyard leaves and returns.
> Life is like that so why not relax?
> Who can stop us from celebrating?"

JUNE 8
London

The above quote was sent to me by my friend Cyndi, and she got it from the Japanese masters. I snack on biscuits and dried fruit that she has sent in a package. These things make me happy. Who can stop us from celebrating? We are all God's children. Let me run barefoot in my mind through green meadows and cool streams. Let me laugh and sing and strum and dance. Stress is for those who have forgotten the Song. Friendship helps me retrace my steps to where I strayed off the path, and I am thankful. I wrote a song today.

JUNE 15
London

It's been a very full week. The sun graces my body with its loving rays, and my spirit soars as I trip through this world of wonder. Some highlights from this week include *The Alchemist* at the Barbican Theater, doing the Tower with Kat and Kelly (whose latest tirade is against spending any money whatsoever. This is hardly possible, but whoever tries to enlighten him is buried in an avalanche of manic apologetic. I admit he is a very creative traveler), dinosaurs with fellow students at the Natural History Museum, road tripping with Kevin (my only English friend. He has shown me several great pubs in the area, and is teaching me to appreciate the finer aspects of James Bond) to his grandmother's estate in Landbourne to visit the White Horse of Uffington, as well as the hilltop where St. George killed his dragon. Kevin's grandmother is gracefully wealthy, and we played tennis and strolled the grounds. We ate dinner with his grandmother, who was without a doubt the epitome of class, and were served hand and foot by those in her employ. I don't have great manners by American standards, and I'm sure I appalled them on more than one occasion. We also visited the stables and the racehorses housed there and sipped Pimms and 7 UP and discussed life until the wee hours of the morning. We ate Haggis. It was glorious.

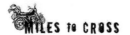

Glory and misery keep company. In the midst of one of the best weeks of my life, something horrible happened. I have been trying to gain the gutzpah to ask Shana Morrison out on a real date (I can't read her at all, which makes me very nervous). This week we were sitting next to each other in our British history class, which meets after lunch. I was trying as hard as is humanly possible not to fall asleep, but to no avail. After lunch I became fatigue itself. So I put my head down on my desk and fell asleep.

I woke up to the sound of a fart. My fart. My after-lunch-right-next-to-the-girl-of-my-dreams-or-at-least-the-girl-with-the-dad-of-my-dreams fart. I couldn't even look at her. I just moaned "Oh dear God." And went back to sleep.

JUNE 27
Bournemouth, England

I am exhausted but happy. It's been about two hours since my last ride, and the time has been spent walking, waiting, smiling, and hoping. I'm in the city of Bournemouth, which is nice, but I'm supposed to be meeting Troy at Land's End tonight, and it's past noon already.

Last night I slept with Irish gypsies—third generation gypsies whose grandparents tinkered around this country in wagons and told fortunes and danced around midnight bonfires. There were about ten families with nice camper trailers, and each male worked construction. There were bits of heavy equipment scattered around this field amid the caravans and cars (including a new Benz and Range Rovers). They were squatting on the land where they had been for the past few weeks, and they planned to move next Wednesday because the court issued an order for their removal. Kevin O'Malley, the foreman by virtue of his owning the steam shovel, told me they usually squat in one place about three weeks if the work is good, and they usually leave at the request of the court. Squatters' rights are such that if they wanted to stay longer, they could, until their case was brought to trial (this is sometimes years). Several children were in each family, and none of them went to school. Few of the adults could read.

All the males in this gypsy clan went to a pub last night, and I was the center of attention as I tried to clear up several misconceptions about America. It was a huge task. I know I did a poor job, because I live in Malibu. I've valeted cars for Chevy Chase and Whoopi Goldberg; I've seen Tom Hanks in a surf shop; Madonna said hello to me as she ran past me on the stairs that lead up from Pepperdine's track to the dorms. ("Madonna!" one of them exclaimed again and again. "Glory be. Madonna! It's not true. Is it? Madonna? Glory!") When I mentioned that I had recently spoken with Van Morrison on the telephone, they almost crapped their pants.

I slept in the large front seat of Kevin's lorry, and this morning his wife Mary cooked us a delicious breakfast. I gave his daughter a quick reading lesson and his dog a quick scratch behind the ears, and then I was off. Their world was barely large enough for a graduate from California as an overnight guest, and it was clear that some of them needed time to digest the way I spoke and the things I said.

I am literally alone in a café that is celebrating its grand opening. The owners are still very optimistic, which makes it easier on me as their sole customer. I've walked a lot today. Love.

I hope my next ride comes quickly.

JUNE 28
Penzance, England

It did. And the next ride as well, and the next and the next and the next. I caught back-to-back rides in convertibles (one BMW and one Alpha Romero) and found myself in Exeter. There I met a beautiful young girl named Naomi, and she took me home and introduced me to the folks, who pampered and fed me. Then off again west (which left me kicking myself going, "Now what was that? I meet this great girl, her parents love and feed me, and I'm leaving?").

Last night it was pitch black as I trooped off the road into a field, but it was lovely. I made camp, unrolled my sack, and cracked open a warm beer that had been in my pack for two days. I leaned back, looked up at the stars, and took a deep breath. I raised a toast to the things I love. I toasted the people I love. I toasted the Lord I love. (I guess I really am a goner. God has wooed me through beauty, through joy, through his Holy Writ, and I'm sunk.) Then I fell asleep.

I woke up with the sun and started walking. A young painter in a van picked me up and took me to a boot sale, which is what they call Flea Markets. There was mostly junk there, but I made a key purchase of a Union Jack Flag. Then I left, and hopped a lift to Penzance, which is where I am now. It's still kind of early Sunday morning, so I guess all the Pirates are still asleep (a landmark comment, and as cheesy as I ever hope to be).

I'm going to St. Ives now. I might have to return through Exeter again for Naomi's sake. Who am I kidding?

Same day. I'm in St. Ives now at a coffee house on the Atlantic. Cobblestones, it's called. But the great thing is how I got here. Two motorcycles were driving by, and one of them had an empty sidecar. I give the driver a glance that says, "You're going where I want to be, and your sidecar is just screaming to hold my bearded wandering self." The driver gives me a look back that says, "I couldn't agree more." Without conversation, I arrive in St. Ives by sidecar. What a long, strange trip it's been.

JULY 4
En route to Stonehenge

I gaze out the train window and watch the English countryside blur by. Floyd lulls my mind to the contemplative, and I recollect the adventures of this past week. It's been eclectically wonderful.

Great discussions with good friends (Troy has been trying to get me to embrace a literal view of the Bible. I asked him if when John the Baptist called Jesus the Lamb of God, he meant that Jesus had white fur and ate grass. I'm not against a conservative view of the Bible's veracity, I just think we can't abandon our minds when we read it), John Malkovich in *A Slip of the Tongue*, Michael Crawford singing Andrew Lloyd Webber tunes, The London Philharmonia, dancing through the a.m. at the Equinox, marathon Monopoly games, and a mud soccer match in a London deluge. Tiffany and I day tripped to Cambridge, ate scones on the river, and watched the punts slice by. For young lords, Cambridge is a rich jewel.

"I believe in living life in the relentless pursuit of genius."
—KELLY RIVERS

"Some dive into the sea, some toil upon the stone. To live is to fly."
—COWBOY JUNKIES

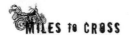

Now I'm trying to get to Stonehenge (that first visit could hardly be called a visit. Budget and indignation prevented me from entering) to attempt to experience the mysterious energies reported there. I'm going to try to sneak in the center of the ring of stones after it gets dark.

The train is being delayed because it is storming and lightning is slicing across the sky, as lightning tends to do. Apparently the electric signals that control the trains have been struck. The sky reels with natural theatrics. It's going to be a good night.

Later. I'm under the eaves of a thick forest that borders the plane adjacent to Stonehenge. Thunder peels from every direction, and the clouds are thick and dark, but so far it is only misting. The plan is to wait until it is pitch-dark and then head for the stones. I'm excited and scared. There are ancient burial mounds littered around the countryside, and one is very near me. The forest cracks and groans its anticipation of the storm. I've had a meal of beans and bread and Tolkien. Jonathon Ronald Reuel is essential for this type of outing, although it's hard to concentrate. There is magic and mystery in the air, and my stomach is fluttering. I think it's about 8:30 p.m., but I can't see my watch. The wind is picking up.

JULY 5
A coffee shop between Stonehenge and London

Next morning. It's going to be near impossible to describe the emotions that last night's dark adventure evoked. As near as I can guess, it was about midnight when I packed up my bag and began my run for the stones. The forest in which I was resting had become pitch black. The sky was an eerie luminous sable, made even more disturbing by the thunder and lightning that ripped and rolled through my being. The wind roared and buffeted so I could hardly walk with my pack on. Things were just a bit surreal.

On the edge of this storm plane, silent fireworks exploded in color. I'm guessing this was somehow to celebrate the Fourth of July, but in England I have no idea who would want to do that. Perhaps that was a good riddance party.

I knew that the Henge was about a mile and a half away, and

that I would have to walk past eight or so burial mounds, keeping them on my right in order to advance in the most secretive manner. Ground visibility was zero. The heavens were engaging in their own fantastic pursuits, but illumination was not one of them. On the far horizon, it was possible to see the outline of trees and other shapes that stood stark against the sky; this was all I could see. I started off in a meandering windblown manner in what I judged to be the right direction. I judged poorly. Fifteen minutes later, I was startled as I saw the mounds of the dead rise up on the plane to my left (I had wanted these on my right). I began to trudge uphill toward them when suddenly a helicopter with a searchlight rose up over the hill and began to scour the countryside with its beam. The police here have begun a war on hippies and witches who use Stonehenge for midnight inspiration (who would want to do that? Okay, guilty as charged). So I dropped down on my face and lay motionless. The helicopter moved on, and I resumed my advance. Slowly. I finally got myself in the right position to approach Stonehenge. The wind died down, and there was no rain, but the lightning still flickered high up in the clouds.

"'But, Ah,' desire still says, 'Give me some food.'"
  —*SIR PHILIP SIDNEY*

Fascinated and terrified, I made my way toward the stones. It took me more than an hour to make sure there were no police patrols. At last, in the dead of night, I stood two hundred feet from Stonehenge looking at the silhouette of the stones against the night. Here I mustered my courage. An eternity later, I was ready. A small fence was my only barrier, and I had grabbed hold of it and prepared to vault myself into the mystic ... when I thought I heard a noise. I crouched down. The blood throbbed in my ears. My imagination had been raging all night, but as I strained to listen, I became sure. I could hear voices mumbling a low chant. I was frozen. And then, accompanying the chant, a small red light was produced ... in the center of the circle of Stonehenge. There was some dark ceremony being performed within the ancient ring of stone. The light swayed back and forth with the low voices and touched upon all of the stones. This went on for five minutes, a minute, an hour; it's hard to say. Then the chanting stopped, and the light was extinguished. I can only guess that the ritual was over and the worshipers were leaving, because someone pulled out a flashlight and left the circle by the darkest path—which meant they were advancing straight toward me. I was slightly alarmed (I felt my hair literally stand on end), and, in a move I am not ashamed of, turned and made a silent but hasty retreat. I saw the beam flicker across me as I beat it toward the road, but I don't think anyone followed me as I fled.

I reached the road in safety and walked a few miles to relax and find a place to sleep. It had started to rain softly. I crawled into a thick grove of trees, spread out my bag, made a peanut butter sandwich, and had a big swig of water. Then I realized I was on the gentle slope of a burial mound. But the night was uneventful, even if I was more skittish than I ever thought it possible for me to be. The wind rustled the trees, and the rain was gentle, and my bag was warm.

I'm still jittering.

"Now I write this from the plane, drinking cheap champagne, and wondering why two people got so far apart."
—JOHN DENVER, "Wish You Were Here"

JULY 10
En route to America

I feel many thoughts and emotions tumbling and bumping inside my cranium, but mainly nostalgia and excitement are doing the waltz. (How can I be nostalgic for a summer not yet ended? What incredible audacity I employ!) I don't really know what to write. The future is now. Potential is infinite. I've finished my undergraduate education, I am unemployed, through wandering Europe for a spell, but undoubtedly starting another American wander. I've got butterflies and indecision, energy and ambition, with very little direction.

The Tao of How ... have I discovered anything true this summer? Have I uncovered verities hidden in dark holes and forests

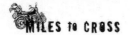

surrounding Stonehenge? Have I climbed mountains of experience and trekked miles down the twisting road of life, only to return devoid of anything tangible, fulfilling? Am I returning to the States with mementos of truth notched in my belt?

What do I know?

I know it is more important to focus on the journey than the destination. Each mile has a wealth of beauty, and new unexplored groves of trees, and unnoticed shades of green, rocks, hills, a bend in the road that tickles the belly at high speed. Destinations are secondary. They are important, but not most important. Like goals, they are necessarily discarded once achieved. The destination, then, is temporary, but the journey goes on.

I know the mystics were right ... there is mystery in the mundane. God is in the moment-by-moment. He is vastly nearer than most people think.

I know there is more romance here than I ever thought possible ... quite enough to keep the Wordsworths and Poes and Falstaffs and Howertons happy for lifetime upon lifetime.

And I know, like sunshine on the back of your neck in July, love beats down upon this place without ceasing.

The bit you play on this stage is of infinite importance. There is a purpose. I'm not sure I know mine yet. But I'm after it with all I've got.

Live.

Love.

You never know your luck.

WANDERLUST TENANT #3

Never Complain.

The third pillar of this Wanderlust Appreciation philosophy is that life itself is a gift. You didn't ask for your lot in life, and you had no control over your entry stall. Nobody did. So nobody (literally) has the luxury of complaining. Of course, work like hell to better your situation, and to get to the places you feel called to go. You have dreams for a reason. Complacency has no quarter here. This is simply a recognition that complaining is the root of all evil. Complaining signals weakness. Complaining tips the hat to a selfish frame of mind. Complaints invite anxiety. Gratitude, on the other hand, destroys it. Being thankful for where you are, who you are, what you are experiencing now ... this is more than a good idea. It's a frame of mind that allows you an odd peace in the face of any circumstance. It's a healthier way to live. Counting your blessings may be hopelessly old-wives'-tale-ish, but it's a good idea nonetheless. Notice things, know yourself, and never complain. These three tenants provide the moral fabric for a life on the road, as well as for the person whose travels consist of venturing to the nearest coffee house and back.

"Complaints wither the fragile fruit tree of your soul. Laughter waters it unto life. Abundance, or a sickness unto death? You choose."
—*JAPHY TINYSPEAR*

"If you are following your bliss, you put yourself on a kind of track that has been there all the while, waiting for you, and the life that you ought to be living is the one you are living. Wherever you are, if you are following your bliss, you are enjoying that refreshment, that life within you, all the time."

—*JOSEPH CAMPBELL*, *The Power of Myth*

PILGRIMAGE FOUR

CENTRAL AMERICA

MAY 10
Guatemala City, Guatemala

I sit in an open-air courtyard with the Indigo Girls singing
sweetly in my ear and my buddy Barry sitting near, and it dawns on
me that we are in Guatemala City. The lure of foreign lands once
again has claimed me. We are staying in a luxurious hotel nearby
(the shower I took was cold, but the bathroom was in my room
and not at the end of the hall), but this place is beautiful and cheap,
running at $7 a head. Now I sit in the courtyard just off our room,
clean and cooled by a sad, warm breeze that wanders lonely through
windows and halls.

I am happy, or at least telling myself that. The clouds today were
thick, and there is a concern that the heat and humidity of this
jungle climate can be achieved without direct sunlight. In other
words, I'm petrified that there is even a slight chance that I'll return
home half as pale-skinned as I arrived. Oh, dear God, no. Please.

I sip room temperature purified water that we made from iodine
tablets, and I am content. A slight paranoia gripped Barry and I
about the various ails we could introduce to our digestive systems

125

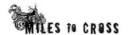

via food and drink. So we decided to just drink beer ("Hey, it's pasteurized!"). But after one in a downtown cantina with horrific mariachi cacophony blaring through a tinny stereo, my headache declared a no-go.

Tomorrow we plan to head to Antigua and enroll ourselves in a Spanish school for a week. Tonight we sleep, for weariness and gentle breezes have issued a mandate, and it is my place to obey.

"Bliss is much more substantial than mere selfishness. In the final analysis, you embrace bliss when you fulfill the reason for your existence."
—*MIKE HOWERTON*

Heartfelt thankfulness for a safe trip. It is a good feeling to offer praises to the One worthy of praise. God has moved past my vague conceptual idea of God, and invaded my life on a personal level. The difference in the quality of my life is substantial. I was diagnosed with asthma a few years ago. Before that diagnosis, my life was fine; I was into sports, I lived an active life, there was no real debilitation. But since the diagnosis, a burden has been lifted. Because of the treatment, when I run, I can breathe. When I hike, I can inhale deeply. When I lay down to sleep, I do it without wheezing or constriction. The point is that it is possible to live either way, with an inhaler or without one. But with is qualitatively better, in ways I previously had never imagined. Life with God is a life that allows me to breathe, to dream, and to run. I feel free, mostly, from the wheezing constriction of my own selfish choices.

MAY 11
Antigua, Guatemala

Barry and I are hanging out in the lush backyard of a Spanish escuela awaiting the arrival of Vincino, the director, who will take us to the home of a local family. Antigua is a thousand times more appealing than Guatemala City, and I can see why this city is the

126

ancient capital. I can also see why they moved the capital from Antigua, simply to preserve its charm. I am at ease wandering the cobblestone streets of this town. My Spanish is indeed sparse, but I am confident that a week in school will do wonders. It seems that there is a lethargy that infects.

Because I'm tired again.

It is still raining. It's black night, and we're in a big room in Angela's home, which is cerca de la escuela. I suppose I could be more mellow, but then I would be dead. Class starts tomorrow a la nueve.

I've just finished *Zorba the Greek* by Kazantzakis. Pretty fiery. A carpe diem classic. Many times I thought of my friend, author Tim Hansel (friend by a definition that includes reading his book, shaking his hand, and having a conversation with him that he would by no possible means remember—that kind of friend, like my other friend, Van Morrison), who is a great zealot of life and who loves God. When I asked him what his favorite book in the world was, he answered *Zorba* without hesitation—not because of his sensualism, Hansel explained, but because of his passion. I wonder if the two concepts aren't closely related. I'm betting they are.

Earlier today my brother Barry and I lived a scene that I would put in the trailer to the movie of my life. It was raining hard, and the shot for the scene would start on the lush green hills that surround Antigua, and then pan down and move toward the town. Through the warm rain, it would follow the rooftops of a tiny side-street, and finally come through the open-aired skylight of a tiny bar. Two students sit at a table reading. One reads *Zorba*, the other a travel guide. On the table are a few empty Gallo bottles; two parrots squawk occasionally from their perch in the corner. I don't really know the significance ... it must be *Zorba*. Life just seems so sweet, my breath was deep and delicious, and I smiled at the thought. There wasn't much else to do. What is the movie of my life about? A man who searches the entire globe for a holy grail, only to find that he carried it in his pack all along.

MAY 14
Antigua, Guatemala

Early morning, and I sit in a Pasteria staring at a steaming cup of café con azucar. No leche hoy. They don't have any. No problema. Kein problem. "No problem" in three languages. Trilingual sophistication. I'm so Renaissance.

Clouds and rain this morning, which is unusual because it usually rains in the afternoon. I sip my coffee from a plastic cup. It is good.

I am completely delighted with the living arrangements. We live in a house with a Guatemalan family (two little girls and their mother) and another student from New Zealand. We get three meals a day, small but delicious native fare. All of this is very pleasing.

The school is great as well. Five hours a day of being grilled in Spanish is not what I'd call a good time, but it is effective. I certainly feel I'm getting my money's worth.

Everything is much cheaper down here, but that is due to a very depressed economy, and a low standard of living prevails. It saddens me, and reinforces some beliefs I hold:

Every player on this stage has a different role to fill.

Each role must be played with zest and gusto.

We are called to serve.

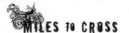
The first belief allows me some peace at the shape of the world as it is; the last allows me a vision of what it can become. Passion is the fuel that allows us to dream. I feel these beliefs must be weighed and balanced in the mind of any compassionate person. I saw a man asleep or in stupor on the street today, literally lying in the gutter. I have no answers; I tried to rouse him, and he wouldn't move even if I had all the answers. I don't know his story. But I know this: In all the world, the saddest thing I see is people making peace with their fetters.

My coffee is gone. It's time for class to begin. Love.

At least it has stopped raining.

This morning
the cloud kisses the mountain;
the rain drifts down
with mournful joy;
the beauty of this quiet causes
a nasty tickle
a sliver in the core
of my soul
and I am vaguely discontented
with my contentment
to be
this morning.

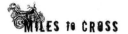

MAY 17

En route to Tikal, Guatemala

It is 5:30 a.m. I'm sitting in the private plane section of the Guatemala City airport, and my stomach is thanking me for the café and raisin buns I've given it. Raisin buns are made from slices of raisin bread folded into quarters. The purpose of this is to trick the stomach into thinking that this is a different meal than the one it got last night. We fly to Tikal in an hour.

Yesterday marked the last day of class, and it was enough.

Yesterday also marked the first day that I've ever seen a live volcano. The experience was tremendously fulfilling. We had to hike miles up the side of a crumbling lava rock volcano. I was the first one up to the top of the mountain, trailing the guide by five minutes or so, and came upon him suddenly as he was cleaning and loading his pistol. I almost wet myself. I thought, sure, this is how they do it: exhaust people by having them climb a mountain and then pick them off one by one as they stagger to the top. Pilfer the goods, and dump the dead into an active volcano. The plan reeks of brilliance.

But they did none of that. The guide explained that there were instances of robbers mugging the guests on the trail, and that was the reason he was packing heat. I was reasonably comforted, although the thought of a showdown between guides and robbers with me in the middle didn't exactly lend itself to peace.

But the volcano itself was intense. Warm ground, loud roaring, lava jetting into the night air and falling as porous rock … it was quite a rush. A wiry dog had come along for the hike and picked his way gingerly through the steaming rocks. Another timeless lesson … there is a hunger of the heart to get close enough to the fire to experience the heat, while attempting to keep from getting seriously burned. Unfortunately, in my life, my flirtations with danger inevitably scorch my soul. Thankfully, God is the great physician.

Later. Today also marked the first day that I've seen a Mayan ruin. Que bonita! The ancient city of Tikal flowers with grace, beauty, and craftsmanship. It was easy to see how a civilized people worked, lived, and worshiped here. I try not to dwell on the human sacrifice that was part of their ritual pleasing arbitrary gods. At one point in my life, I counted all religious worship identical. Now there is simply no way for me to do that. Worship has historically been based upon two things: the values of the god worshiped and the values of the culture worshiping. But no one really has any reason to make the mistake that all worship carries the same value, or that God is the same god in all cultures. There IS one God, and He loves every culture on this globe. He does look for sacrifice, but not by the death of a vestal virgin. He looks for the sacrifice of a life that is lived in pursuit of Him, in embrace of His love, and in invitation to others. And He requires nothing of us that He did not first model to us. I think that is why I can't ignore Him. He isn't high and mighty up on a throne indifferent to the sufferings of humanity. He enters into that suffering; He models a radical love of giving life away for others. His crucifixion provides

salvation. His resurrection showcases victory. And His indwelling in the hearts of His followers provides purpose and power for life on this dusty plane, and preparation for eternity on a higher one.

Barry and I climbed to the top of as many temples and houses that would hold us. I've never seen a ruin more pristine, more complete. I also saw two howler monkeys and toucans a-plenty.

But right now, let's face it: I'm sweltering. In a swelter. I have become heat and humidity. This city of Flores (Santa Elena) in which we are staying swelters an impressive climax to any other swelter I have known. The night is sultry. Sweat drips from my face as I write. It is hot. Africa hot. Were you born on the sun? It is that hot.

Traveling with my buddy Barry is very cool. I dig conversations with him, and I love traveling with him. He is a mellow planner, very practical, and I'm letting him do all the planning. He tells me what we want to do, and then we do it. I'm able to communicate in Spanish more easily than he is, so we've got a good thing going.

I'm giving Barry one minute to finish his cold shower. Then I'll throw his butt out.

Because I'm sweltering.

MAY 18
Naranjo, Guatemala

Today we leave Guatemala by boat. From the tiny town of Naranjo, we are taking a boat up the river through the lush jungle, and we are thinking that it is going to be good, kind of like the jungle cruise at Disneyland ... only bigger. In fact, that is a theory I'm working on ... that life is like Disneyland, only bigger. And the attendants don't clean the park as well. (Okay, this is a shining example of a stupid theory.)

For the second morning in a row, we were up before 4 a.m. to catch a bus. A five-hour bus ride in the dust and bounce of a third world jungle does not invite sleep. I'm tired. But the dust, and the humidity, and the exhaustion—hey! That's what I came for! And beauty does surround, although mixed continually with squalor and poverty. It's a wiser version of me that shall return to the comfort of the States.

Barry and I had a good discussion last night about Truth. Absolute Truth. It was edifying for both of us. Barry is a good thinker. At times I think I'm the one with faith. At times I think he has more faith than is possible. He simply hesitates to put legs to it. Faith, at the end of the road of speculation, forces a leap. Far easier (I know this much) to wander the road of speculation again ... singing, "I still haven't found what I'm looking for." I pray for the courage to leap. To live leaping daily.

Barry was asking me about my motivations for faith, and I told him that joy and transcendence have always motivated me. I simply have found that knowing God and being His provide more joy and transcendence than I have found through anything else. I've known what it is like to be my own god, serving my whims and appetites unto exhaustion, and what I realize in my moments of clarity is that

my tiny universe buckles under the burden of serving myself. I am a horrible master, goading myself toward oppression and depression with every act of self-gratification. So I quit! I walked away from god-hood, which is only easy to do in the presence of the Real, the Authentic, the Being-One. In the presence of the Divine, my show is unmasked, my folly revealed, my charade named! And joyfully, I'm set free! My misguided devotion to self I offer willingly to the only One in the universe worthy of my devotion! God Himself, how wonderful! God, how liberating! And the blessed irony of it all is that when I move my satisfaction off of the throne, and instead focus on just walking this road of devotion for Him, with Him, by Him ... then my satisfaction creeps up on me with a shy smile and embraces me unlooked for. When satisfaction is the goal, it eludes like the shine of glory at the far edge of your peripheral vision. In those moments, Mick Jagger's right: I can't get no. But when loving Him is the goal, the dam bursts, and satisfaction floods in like so much grace.

"I can't get no satisfaction." —*MICK JAGGER*

I once heard a preacher compare the human life to the migration of the monarch butterfly. The migration begins in North America and leads a meandering course down into Argentina. He said that we too have a migration to make. The most important thing, he said, is to persevere. Inevitably, we meander off-course. The trick is to meander right back on-course. We can trust God for guidance, because, like the butterfly, He is the one who calls us. He is calling us home. He ought to know the way.

Love.

As I close this entry, I am overwhelmed by gratitude. Thanks to the Lord of the jungle. Thanks to the Lord of the dance, the Lord of my life. Thank you, Sir. Thank You for my clean body and my full belly. Thank You for a ceiling fan in this room in the backwaters of southern Mexico. Thank You for the adventure thus far and the adventure to

A foolish consistancy
is the hobgoblin of
little minds,
It's been said,
with great self-confidence
and gusto.
But a humble, thoughtful
consistancy,
mighty be
like the migration of a Monarch;
Bold, bespeckled, fluttering,
fragile,
fraught with danger,
disaster,
distance,
and yet,
in the end,
filled with a quiet
ultimate
triumph.

be. Thanks for salvation, which is a continuing process all around me, which lifts me like a rising tide, which cleanses shame even as I write, and thank You for Your friendship.

> I love You, even despite myself.
> Tomorrow is another five o'clock morn.
> Warm beer is also a gift.
> I miss traveling with Toph.

MAY 21
Puerto Escondido, Mexico

We've found ourselves in the amazing Margaritaville paradiso-type village of Puerto Escondido. Wonderfully laid-back and beautiful, with great surf right out in front ("The most gnarly beach break on the planet, dude," says a surfer emerging from the wash with half a board still leashed to his ankle). We are staying in a cool little cabana on the beach. It has electricity, water, a fan, a fridge, a stove, a shower, a toilet, two beds under mosquito netting, and a front porch on which we eat and sling our hammocks. For eight dollars a night, this place is fine. Very fine.

The travel here has been tough. Plane, boat, train, bus, car, and taxi, and now we are going to just stop for a few days. Relax. Surf. Wash my underwear, and let it dry by the window.

Today we pick up our boards.

Barry and I continue metaphysical discussions.

MAY 22
Puerto Escondido, Mexico

It is a brilliant morning of sun, sand, and surf, but we two parrot-heads are moving a bit slow. It was a grand night. We made friends with the waiters at one of the restaurants on the sand, and by the end of the night, they were joining us for Souza and Pacifico. We closed the place down, and now Barry and I are moving quietly, deliberately, as if we might break.

The surf continues to be wickedly violent. If it doesn't improve, or if we can't find a better break, we may head south ahead of schedule.

"Wasting away again in Margaritaville." —*JIMMY BUFFETT*

Later. A mellow night of reflection in my hammock in the cool darkness of a coastal evening listening to R.E.M. I write by candlelight. I think of Ghormley Meadow and people I love. I think of a girl I don't yet know. I wonder who she is and why I love her so much. I'm reading odd fantastic stories by F. Scott Fitzgerald.

I glance down at my arm in the light of the candle. Dark, chiseled, glistening with humidity, veins raised leading shadow. I write this in thankfulness. The human body is a gift; it is art; it is miracle.

The ocean is hypnotic and addictive. I am held in its sway, listening for a message in the waves, but what I hear is the heartbeat of the world.

We have our boards. Tomorrow we hit a cove Barry and I scouted out today by hiking and sweating along a ridge until we stumbled upon an emerald feast. It looks like the point break creates a long left

shoulder to ride. Tomorrow will be a nice day.

MAY 25
San Salvador, Mexico

It's been a strange, strange day. "What a long, strange trip it's been." I'm sitting in a bus station in San Salvador waiting for Barry to return with changed monies. If he succeeds, victory, and we will have upgraded seats on a bus to San Jose. If he doesn't, failure, and we not only have no ride, but we have no way of paying for a place to stay tonight, either.

But the day has been golden, green, lush, with cool breeze in open windows and cool rain upon outstretched palms. Tunes nostalgic beckon memory, and I've been in love all day. When the road rolls under your feet and the wind is in your face and sad song breaks your heart, there is a mad connection with truth. Pascal says, "The heart has its reasons that reason knows not." He's right.

It has to do with love.

I thank God for this gift. This trip is not lacking in the un-expected, and just at this instant, I think that is brilliant.

Taxi drivers lean against their cars and talk excitedly outside. They are as excited as political activists. Perhaps they are.

When we left Puerto Escondido, we left at night. I was trying to sleep on the bus, as was most everybody on board. But I woke up to see the driver leaning out of the bus, using a flashlight to see the road as he drove. I guess his headlights had gone out. And I thought about stressing for about a minute. Then I thought, what the heck, he's probably done that a hundred times. And I fell back asleep.

Barry returned with no luck, and now it's night, and we two travelers rest in beds provided by Barry's MasterCard. Tomorrow we explore San Salvador, and that is a good thing, and then we head toward Costa Rica, and that is a very good thing.

Right now I'm struck with the realization that things spiritual have often invaded my material existence. When I was still in school, I had two experiences that cannot be understood as anything other than spiritual. In the first, I saw a golden lady. Or I saw an angel. Either way, the peace that remained throughout the afternoon was thick, like the smell of a chocolatier's den. Pepperdine is surrounded by steep hills (a mountain biker's paradise), and on a bright afternoon, several students from our Heidelberg program had gathered for fondue. (Fondue? Who did we think we were?) The apartment we were in had an excellent view of the hills that hemmed our campus into place, and it was there, surrounded by the laughter of friends, I slipped out of time. As I gazed from the third story window, I saw a lady, beautiful beyond words, surreal, and serene as the foundation of all things good, and she ran, if running you could call it. Straight down the hillside she flowed, white robes like wings carrying her through the bracken, a Shakespearian maid running at incredible speed, and yet completely, as it were, in slow motion. In that timeless instant, I desperately wanted to know her, to know what errand she sped toward, to know that whoever had sent her also had sent word for me. I remember forgetting to breathe. "What are you looking for?" A voice startled me back among the living, and it was Toph. "There," I said, but the hillside I pointed to was empty.

In the second experience, Jesus embraced me. My concept of sin was still being formed (as "thoughts or actions destructive to self or others," which is not a bad definition), and I woke up late on a Sunday afternoon sick with it. My soul was filthy. What festered was the whisper that I had lived here before, that I had always lived here, that this sickness wasn't passing, that it was unto death. I felt hopeless. Life was hopeless. I was weary with the knowledge that I could not change my life. I was haunted by this: If I could have changed, I would have changed already. Instead, I floundered in a mire of my own creating. I took a walk on Little Dume with my dog. The beach was deserted; the sky spit rain, November. I remember looking out at the kelp forest swaying in the bay. It looked so peaceful, so appealing. The chaos and guilt and paranoia that was my life longed for the gentle sleep that the water promised. "Swim out, swim down," the siren song played, "we'll hold you, we'll help you." In this moment of life without hope or future, these were the voices that urged my destruction.

Instead, I looked up. I could see the raindrops falling from a great height. I spoke out loud to the sky, to myself, to the God who turned out to be nearer than myself, and I said, "If you are real, and if you want me, then now would be a good time to tell me." It was a prayer heaved skyward from the edge of a cliff. And then Jesus embraced me.

"There are more things in heaven and earth, Horatio, Than are dreamt of in your philosophy." —*HAMLET*, Shakespeare

I wish it was a Spielberg moment, clouds swirling, becoming celestial arms, a voice thundering from the heavens, sand-crabs joining the dolphins in singing "Jesus Christ, Superstar," light all around. Externally, nothing happened but the fall of rain. Internally, Jesus held me. Deep inside, it was His whisper I heard; it was His love that told me, "I have been waiting so long for you." All an observer would have seen was a weeping man standing, looking up at the rain. All I saw was Him. All I felt was Him, providing hope in my hopelessness. Where guilt had been tyrant, His grace brought freedom. Where I saw no future, His future for me was good. Being held by Him is good. Walking with Him is good. In the last year or so, I've not found that being a believer is always fun or easy. I can't find anywhere in the Bible where it promises that. But I have found that it is always good. It's good to be His. I'm sure that is because He is Good.

Weariness clouds the intellect, and it's time to drift.

MAY 26
Capital of El Salvador

Barry and I cool our heels in a room with a fan immediately next to the bus station running the bus that heads toward San Jose tomorrow at 5 a.m. I have no idea why there are so many 5 a.m. days on this trip, but it may destroy me.

Today we maneuvered through this city like conquerors. Once we got our bearings, we found we owned the place, so we went to the zoo.

It was good, the zoo, but the leopards looked hot, and the hippo stayed under his murky pond. The monkeys clasped our fingers with their tiny able hands, and some sort of connection was made, but not an ancestral one. It was more like an essay on freedom and being.

Moby Dick sits at my side, and the leviathan looks as forbidding as ever.

Yesterday I spent time in thought over the toast at Christopher and Jen's wedding. I love them so much that this was a very pleasant endeavor. They don't plan to wed until October, but I'd like to be prepared.

Included in the price of this room (which is $6 a night) is pure, cold water for drinking. This is another reason I thank God.

My surfboard stares at me from the corner and wonders if I will ever make it proud. Who knows? The future is bright and hazy as ever, and like Joyce Carol Oates, I don't have the answers to where am I going, where have I been. But I have considerably more hope than she did.

I think of Sage, and of Cyndi, and even of the girl I don't yet know, and I wonder if it takes a schizophrenic to be in love with them all. Am I psycho? Or is this just what twenty-two years old looks like?

I choose virtue. It is the choice with eternal benefits. A person with integrity never has to hide, or even have a very good memory. "He was a good man," may they say about me. And may it be true.

Much later:

"It's possible!" I shout.

"What's possible?" Barry hollers through his headphones.

"Anything's possible!" I shout back through the music, and I'm right.

The embrace of gloom is a choice. The existential mishmash of doom is a choice, not a proven, not a given. I, for one, refuse to accept it.

The Seattle grunge is negativism incarnate, and my denial is based upon more than a moral stepstool. It is based upon the pragmatic embrace of an optimism that works. That's both fun and productive. Enough. The truth is non-negotiable. Even despite myself.

MAY 27
Nicaraguan Border, en route to San Jose

> **Coincidence**
> n.
> 1. a coinciding 2 an accidental, but seemingly planned, occurrence of events, ideas, etc. at the same time

I don't really want to remember this day. We've been sitting for a year and a day on this bus that is stopped at the Nicaraguan border, and I'm pretty sure it's hot enough to melt lead in here. There is a guy molding coins in the back of the bus.

Sweat runs off of me. This is as close to hell as anyone needs to get.

It is much later now and ever so much cooler. We are about to crash for the night in a room right next to the bus, which is still taking us to San Jose. I've just hopped out to the shower, and when the fan blows on me, it is truly refreshing.

Last night was a brilliant night of philosophy, theology, and budgeted beers. Barry and I switched tapes on the Walkman, and listened to each other's respective outlooks on life. His tape depressed me, and mine made him want to dance.

Last year when I was in London, I met a girl who is in the Peace Corps. She was the daughter of the visiting faculty, and was taking a break from saving the world to travel England with her parents. We didn't hit it off, but I was interested in her descriptions of the Peace Corps, and in what she had to say about living in Guatemala. There is within me a huge desire to make a difference in the world, to point people toward hope, and to live significantly. In my conversations with friends, and those I meet traveling, I know I'm not alone in this. Anyway, yesterday, as Barry and I were traveling through an out of the way corner of Guatemala, riding on a bus with several families, chickens, and pigs, this same girl climbed aboard. I was blown away. I yelled out, "I know you!" The funny thing was that she didn't seem interested at all in talking to me, which is exactly how she treated me in London, now that I think about it, so at least she's consistent, even with the world being as small as it undoubtedly is.

This reaffirms my belief that there is simply no coincidence. Suddenly I'm remembering two years ago, when Toph and I decided to take a road trip up to see the Grateful Dead play in Oakland, and we hit San Francisco for a night of exploration before the show. Our plan was to sleep in my truck outside of the Presidio, but before we crashed, we wandered the Pier 39/Ghiradelli's Square area. We headed to one of the restaurants near the wharf to grab a drink, and our waitress turned out to be Barry's sister. I was floored. I had no idea she was back in the States; the last report I had heard was that she was wandering through Central America on her own. So that night, besides receiving the delightful surprise of unlooked for connection and discounted appetizers, a desire to explore Central America was birthed in my heart. And now I'm here with Barry. Life is so peculiar. Has there ever been a coincidence? Or is there just love? I know bad and crazy things "just happen" as well ... a man stubs his toe and falls, not to the ground, but through the hole in the ground where the men are re-routing the sewage lines, and breaks both his wrists. However, he happens to grasp a locker key in the mud at the bottom. When he is healed, he finds the appropriate locker, opens the key, and unwittingly releases a disease that kills him and the twelve nuns standing near, praying. It happens. I'm just saying it stands side-by-side with the good and crazy things.

The land that passes by outside the windows of the bus stretches and spirals green in more shades than my eye can recognize. Humidity continues to stick to me.

"And with a great voice he said: 'When love beckons to you, follow him, Though his ways are hard and steep. And when his wings enfold you yield to him, Though the sword hidden among his pinions may wound you.'"—*KAHLIL GIBRAN*

MAY 28
San Jose, Costa Rica

San Jose, Costa Rica, is an oasis of peace and friendliness. Geared toward tourism, Barry and I were able to gather the necessary bus info, buy my return plane ticket to Guatemala City, and find a cheap place to stay all in the space of a half hour. Tomorrow we hit the beach for a week.

I have yet to pen my thoughts comparing this travel experience to others I've had. The reason: Comparisons are odious, says Kerouac, and I know he is right. This is such a different place, different climate, with such a different travel companion, that this experience is, how shall I say? Different. We have successfully traveled the length of Latin America (excluding Panama), have lost cash at every border, and have been alternately disappointed and delighted with every place we've seen.

We've seen a lot by bus. We've spent a lot of time on the bus. Central America is much bigger than Barry or I imagined. Much longer. More bumps.

The only disaster that occurred (okay, I don't think it qualifies as a disaster) is that our water leaked in my pack and soaked this journal. Now it is falling apart. I don't mind so much. It is easier to believe that I brought it on this swelter fest journey through the jungle.

Costa Rica es muy rica, gorgeous green, with the sweet, cool, wet air to breathe. The suffocating heat of yesterday is a dim, dim memory that fades even as I write.

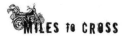

MAY 29

San Jose, Costa Rica

"I thought it was 'If a body catch a body,'" I said. "Anyway, I keep picturing all these little kids playing some game in this big field of rye and all. Thousands of little kids, and nobody's around—nobody big, I mean—except me. And I'm standing on the edge of some crazy cliff. What I have to do, I have to catch everybody if they start to go over the cliff—I mean if they're running and they don't look where they're going I have to come out from somewhere and catch them. That's all I'd do all day. I'd just be the catcher in the rye and all. I know it's crazy, but that's the only thing I'd really like to be. I know it's crazy."
—*HOLDEN CAUFIELD*, J.D.Salinger, *Catcher in the Rye*

I woke up this morning in the Tiralinda Hotel to the sounds of breakfast and the murmur of the voices of travelers. I dine like a king on black coffee and plain toast.

This is a very Euro-hostel type place. It is full of young travelers, and last night we went to a jazz club with two Englishmen and two beauties from Norway. The music was very interesting: a piano man and a violinist, both giving it all they had, their artistic forms convulsing to the rhythm of the mood, and every once in a while emitting wails and shrieks they found appropriate. Interesting, but I wasn't about to drop cash to buy their tape. Is passion enough to make it? Is talent? Or is the point to sing your song and play your role for all you're worth, and then be content regardless because of the sheer honor to sing and to play in the first place?

Time for more toast. I'd like to get my money's worth.

There is a polite disinterest that travelers have when they meet one another in hostels. Everyone wants to share about the amazing places they've been. They would much rather share than listen. Each one likes to make it seem that their destinations, their stories, their experiences are the most amazing. Everyone wants to tell, and nobody wants to ask. I'm no different. The best travel experience I ever had with a fellow hosteller was in Figueres, Spain, with a girl from Israel. We didn't drink together, and we didn't sleep together; we merely traveled together. Politely. For two days. Largely in silence. I don't think either of us could think of much to say. But the silence itself was a form of kindness. I can't even remember her name. But God, you know it, and I ask your blessing upon her life today. Thanks.

MAY 30
Jaco, Costa Rica

Finally we have succeeded in reaching our destination: Jaco, Costa Rica. We are staying at Chuck's place (owned of course, by Mike) about one hundred yards away from a fun, mellow beach break that we surfed today. This place is ideal. The people have been generous. The literacy in this country is high, and the litter problem is low. If poverty is a major issue, it's a hidden one.

The place we are staying is full of Americans and Canadians who are caught in the laid-back attitude of Jaco, and who are at least interesting. There is a group here from Texas that looks like they don't know glam metal died. I've not heard cowboy-surf lingo before, but oh, have I been missing out.

Tomorrow we head out to surf early.

MAY 31
Jaco, Costa Rica

I woke up this morning sick to my soul, and not from too much beer. Something is wrong with me; my spirit is dark and out of focus; I'm not connected to what is real. I'm scared. Dear God, forgive me. Please. My sins have been neither bold nor blasphemous. They have been sins of apathy, which may be worse. Eliot rants, "We are the hollowmen, we are the dead men." Lord, please fill this hollow man with Your Spirit. With love, grace, and peace. I choose You, God. Help me make that choice real as I live.

Sweet Jesus.

I read the story of the prodigal son again today, and I began to weep. You are so beautiful. Your grace is so wonderful, so rich, so extravagant. It woos me, when I am weary of myself and sickened, when I have had enough of my pretense, of my shows of goodness, of my wallowing in the pigsty. I come walking back to You with my head down, practicing my apology, rehearsing my contrite heart again and again, my embarrassed spirit wondering if yet again, You'll forgive me, if just this once more, You'll relent, and as I mumble contrition to myself, I suddenly understand that You are sweeping me off of my feet; Your arms are around me; You are clothing me with Your own garments of holiness; the ring, You place the ring on my finger, and I'm appalled. You can't do that, Lord. I'm not worthy. I shouldn't even be one of Your slaves ...

"Shh, Shh," You whisper. "This is home. This is where you belong. Here is where you are alive. Here is where you are found. Enter in, and let's sup, let's celebrate, let's reign together." And I'm undone. The scandal of grace is so beautiful, it wounds me with sweetness. In humble gratitude I offer my thanks. Thank You. Thank You.

Thank You, my Jesus.

Amen.

The day has dawned
resplendent with possibility
like the wide curious eyes of a newborn
like a slate wiped clean without memory
like a sailor's first sight
    of unexpected landfall.
And there is excitement in the
    crisp morn air
that reaches deep within
    my belly
to the very thing which is
    me
    and cries,
    Dance!
And I smile, and my eyes
    fill with tears,
muttering quiet
    as I shuffle, yes
    yes,
if only I knew how.

> full
> adj.
> 1 having in it all there is space for; filled
> 2 having eaten all that one wants
> 3 having a great deal or number (of)
> 4 complete, satisfied

"I have come that they may have life, and have it to the full."
—*JESUS*, John 10:10b

JUNE 1
Jaco, Costa Rica

My surfing is better and worse than it ever has been. It is harder to get outside than I remember, but it is easier to catch waves than I remember as well. And there is something to be said for the inner exuberance that comes standing up on the shoulder of a four-foot wave of glass and taking it for miles.

It is the definition of a gift.

There is a dog here named Jack, squat white with black splotch who in manner and expression reminds me of my pup Ashley, and it makes me smile. Dogs too, are a gift. God's gift to the insecure.

For the past two nights, we have dined in the home of Emily, a matriarch who makes huge meals for the surfers staying in nearby cabanas. Both tasty and delicious.

They have a saying down here that they use to answer the greeting, "Que pasa?" It is "Pura vida." Pure life. What's up? Pure life. I like it. It is encouraging and uplifting. It reminds of what should forever remain a priority.

Last night Barry and I had a discussion with a young philosophy student from Canada. Several naïve and idealistic statements were uttered by the boy, and I pounced heavily. I was arrogant, and I was better at pseudo-intelligent diatribe than he was. Later I apologized.

The exercise of argument is a ruthless pursuit, a mental masturbation. Last night it got sticky.

JUNE 2
Jaco, Costa Rica

It is dawn, and the first smiles of sunlight have reached me. I'm up at 5, and I don't have to be. What cruel malice is being enacted upon my sleep patterns? Perhaps I was meant to greet this new day. The ocean sings a song that purifies. I watch the waves, and I think about surf and try to mentally improve. The fog that hovers in the dark on this coast is warmed and lifts into nothingness. Tiny crabs scurry in and out of the mountains and valleys of my footprints. I only watch because I'm fascinated. It's time to see if Mario has begun to serve coffee.

JUNE 3
Jaco, Costa Rica

The most tremendously noisome thunder accompanies the most dangerously close lightning to add thrill to the hurricane-like condition that exists here this afternoon. Like fools, we were surfing in the rain until it began to get really nasty. Then a sizzle, and a terrible crack of thunder, and everyone flinched at the sound and the light, and Barry said a blue arc actually leaped through his ankle. The only other person who saw it (Barry's contact with sheer energy) also said that he himself had been struck in the head. So I'm not quite sure his testimony is valid.

It's been a fun day and a fun trip, and tomorrow I wing to Guatemala City and the next day to California to laugh with my loved ones. My hair is long, long, and my beard is oh so scraggly, but I like it. I feel like an apostle. I've started reading an interesting book called the *Illuminatus*. It's horse-urine to the thirsty, but interesting to say the least. I'm also mid-way through the Inklings. As he did Ahab, *Moby Dick* has eluded me yet again. Somebody thinks it's a great book.

The rain falls like it's being poured from a pitcher.

JUNE 4
Guatemala City, Guatemala

I'm in the Aurora Airport in the city, and I'm drinking coffee and eating (of all things) chocolate cake. Chocolate cake! What the heck am I doing eating chocolate cake in an airport in Guatemala? Don't ask me. I don't know.

I ate it fast (to destroy the evidence), and now I'm sipping coffee. Nice. The place I'm staying is right next to the airport, and I have canvassed the surrounding neighborhoods looking for a place to appease the hunger and pen a few words, but to no avail. So I wandered back inside up to the coffee shop and looked at the glass display and pointed, "Como esta estos?" The chocolate things? Oh, they're good. And before I even know what's going on, I'm sitting on a terrace eating cake and having it too.

This life is so strange. Pura vida.

Later now, and I'm sitting outside in a park, and there is a slight
sprinkle on head and page, and I've decided it is one of the loneliest
of days. But a good lonely. A young couple walks arm-in-arm through
the park and are whistled and called at by the workers lounging
against a fence.

Life persists in any and all circumstances, and there is laughter found
on every corner of the globe (not that globes have corners), but there
are tears as well, and as S.E. Hinton says, things are rough all over.
What can we do to serve?

Love.
Live pure.
Smile.
Give of yourself.
Laugh.
Cry.
Feel.
Think.

Search for truth with all that is within you. Find and convey
the peace that comes from this. Faith and hope do abide, and in
abundance, thank God. But the greatest of these is love. Have I done
these things on this quest for Pacific surf? Almost, maybe. On my best
day. I smiled and loved, but I may have enjoyed too many Gallos to
live pure. My thinking is shoddy at best, but I've attempted the good
life. At least I've wanted to attempt it. The last night of our stay, Barry
and I were accosted by a prostitute in Jaco, toothless, aged, unstable,
but we cared for her by purchasing a meal for her, speaking kindly to
her, and abusing her not at all. Is that a giving of self? Maybe. Does
it make a difference? Certainly. Is there always room to do more?
Undoubtedly.

The sun is setting. My hair and beard are long and unkempt. Barry
has been calling me a monk for many months, ever since I moved up
to Ghormley. Today he elevated me from that status to that of prophet.
I'll do my best to live up to the post. The purple and red flowers here
love the quiet sprinkle God provides. So do I.

Somewhere along this Central American jaunt ... beach, jungle, volcano ... somewhere it hit me—joy. Like a double-shot of espresso, my heart pounding in my throat, I wanted to run, so I did; I wanted to sing, so I did; I wanted to fly, and maybe I did, but it was because I was thankful, I was so thankful, I AM so thankful. I couldn't stop saying thank You, thank You, thank You, God, thank You for loving this wandering pilgrim and for loving all wandering pilgrims, and experiencing only His love back, more and more, a Divine Yes, Yes, Yes, affirming love, affirming life, affirming myself, Yes, even affirming the journey, because in the final analysis, it all works together for His glory, Yes, and can I live for His glory? Yes, and can I point others toward His glory? Yes. And Yes. And YES.

My heart is bursting, and it's all I can do to keep my feet on the ground. Life.

Is there anything else?

there is a great power
that brings friends together
that fuels laughter
that creates intimacy
that heals broken souls
Love

It's the power that created
life itself
and to embrace it
is to succeed at the very essence
of being
love
This power, despite its greatness, remains
unobtrusive
like dew on the petals of roses
writing
pristine in beauty droplet
for an observant spirit to leap with joy
but without promotion,
allowing itself to be neglected,
forgotten.
choose.
live.
love.

JUNE 5
En route to California

Homeward bound, but just barely. The departure tax is ten bones from Guatemala. And this bewildered monk has at the end of it all $7 U.S. and two Quetzales. Things are looking bleak. But for the kindness of United Representative Mr. Martin, my baggage would have arrived alone in Los Angeles.

I admit: I'm sick of it. I'm sick of petty taxes and fees and semi-legitimate ways of extorting money from travelers. I've left Guatemala three times now, and this is the first time I can recall it being $10. But enough of this whine. Tonight I shall sup at my parent's home. Parental compassion cures a multitude of travel ills.

And if I sound unhappy, then I've given the wrong impression. Fiercely happy might be more appropriate. Like pepper in an empty cupboard. And didn't I write yesterday that love is all you need (Beatles theology)? It is still true. But boldness has a place too, and that might be what traveling is about.

If Sage is back in town, it just might be time for a raucous reunion.

Perhaps the Tao of How might not subscribe to completion. But then again, neither does life. Or love, for that matter.

WANDERLUST TENANT #4:

Love.

The final tenant of Wanderlust Appreciation is simply: love. It is a continual challenge to see that others are a gift to your life. When you notice things, you will be able to see others as individuals, as brothers and sisters, and you will begin to see their needs. When you know yourself, you will be able to drop your defense tactics, allow yourself to draw near, and allow others near to you. When you embrace a no complaints attitude, your attention shifts off yourself; not neglecting self, but merely forgetting self. Serving is the final antidote to selfishness. Serving is love's body. Service is love's hands. Look at

Mother Teresa, for crying out loud. Joy is a by-product. It is what happens when you get out of the way. Love. Every life you touch is significant. Every life is infinite. What you do matters. Love. Of course you will be confronted with needs that far outdistance your ability to solve. You can't do everything. So let yourself off that hook. You aren't the savior of the world, thank God. Don't worry about doing everything. You can't. Just do something. Notice things. Know yourself. Never complain. Love.

Like I said at the outset, it's barely a shell of a philosophy. But I'd put money on the fact that it has never been lived. Not consistently. Well, once maybe. But that was two thousand years ago. It's time we take another crack at it.

"Love is your soul's breath, your soul's sustenance, your soul's flight, your soul's triumph. Love is your purpose. Love is your Savior. Embrace Love, and truly live."

—JAPHY TINYSPEAR

EPILOGUE

EPILOGUE

me

The bard within so often
quiet I wonder if
he is indeed there
or
if I'm just lazy.

My bride
With strand of hair resting
   upon satin cheek
eyes closed and the rise and fall
  of breath, slow with method
     you sleep,
   and in such a state
seem statuesque, flirting with Hellenism
  a goddess of youth or beauty
     or peace
   sculpted with grace at the hand
    of a gentle Master.

in such times as this, I gaze silent
   I cannot other
my heart broken again and again
by the waves of love dashing and crashing it
   against the rocky shore
the rage of a rising tide
    boiling, roaring
    pounding within
 I breathe your air
   I'm still.

would that I could prove my love,
charging in, rescuing, rushing giants
        slaying dragons,
a young rain-soaked Furey singing to his death
        But no.
a tamer season we enjoy
        bittersweet
I kiss your cheek, satin, and leave for work.

165

My babe
Parked again on my hill
the day is gray and
glorious
I stare at my mountain
shrouded with wonder
alive with possibility
and I am glad.
A windmill turns
the creek moves quietly
along its path
and my lungs hurt
from breathing in so
much
beauty.

But more lovely than
    green mountain,
more graceful than
    bird flight,
more poetic than
    creeksong,
are the rosé lips
of my baby girl
    parted sweet in yawn
    and stretch
borging comfort in her
    blanket bed
asleep in the nook
    of my elbow.

I'm sitting here in a classroom (finishing my Master's degree in theology) nine years later, and my life has obviously changed. I've fallen in love with a beautiful woman (the one I was in love with before I ever met her), and somehow have convinced her to be my wife. An angel of a daughter has been born to us, and she amazes me with the simplest of miracles: herself. My son is all boy, a roly-poly bear cub bursting with energy, and I can't believe that this, the relational equivalent of winning the lottery, is my life. My friends Christopher and Jen have married each other, Dean has spent time working with the Peace Corps in Tibet. Barrett T. is a public defender, and a good one. I have become in the years between, somewhat surprisingly perhaps, a minister. Because of my wanderings, I can see both sides of many issues. But I'm in. Joyfully IN. I don't take myself too seriously, but I do take God seriously. It's been a while since I've enjoyed one, but I can understand a love of a finely brewed ale. (In John, chapter two, Jesus turns water into wine, and I believe it. Like all good gifts, excess perverts, and so with this gift, as with most others, caution and balance are advised.) I teach. I preach. I systematically fail to pound a pulpit or thump a Bible. I do weddings. I work with college students, because for me, college represented a monumental journey. My goal is to launch others toward heroism, toward life as

the adventure they instinctively know it to be. In regards to how I feel about God, my convictions have become clear. Life has changed. And while on most counts I maintain a real sense of contentment, there is a lonely gnawing within my heart upon occasion ... it is the hungering for a wander. Not tourism, but travel at its core, exploration of culture, beauty, and life. A celebration of freedom. Backpacking. Hitchhiking. Catching midnight trains and waking up in distant lands.

It's been cold lately, and it's January, and yesterday morning I caught the scent of something in the early crisp air that took me back to the Moorhaus, back to Heidelberg. It was the clean diesel smell of a fresh bread truck making its rounds. And I began to think of breakfasts there. Indigo Girls with cappuccino, butter croissants with melted cheese. I remember stepping outside in the mornings, and beginning the long walk down, down the front walkway to the gate, down the hill past Henniger Pub, down the Hauptstrasse to the classrooms. I remember that even the smell and shape of the classrooms made me feel like a scholar—inflated my sense of intellect, freedom, and self-importance.

Good classes too—literature, art history, and German. I took the Hitler class as well, vicariously, through discussions with friends in pubs and train compartments. There is nothing like reading Keats, or Goethe, and glancing outside the train window at the romance of the

countryside as it glides by. There is nothing like studying a piece of art, and then finding it by chance (which is how I found everything) in a museum. This happened often, and yet I will never forget the immensity of this realization as it hit me in the Musee D'Orsay in Paris, walking past walls and walls of Monet, Renior, Picasso, Seurat.

But my fondest memory of a typical day was, without a doubt, our break times between class. A group of us would hurry down to Café Sieben, conscious of time and our breath visible, to partake of cappuccinos, which I learned to drink there. Or, if the hunger pangs hit early, we would find the pretzel vendor and eat our steaming prize quickly, burning our mouths.

Lunch breaks, we would head to the Mensa at the university, and if we were feeling wealthy, we would stop at the bakerei to score a domfneudl for einmark fufsig. If I think for a moment, I can feel my warm roll stowed in my coat pocket, and the anticipation of tasting its salt and butter joy.

I can still feel the air on my face as I walked along the cold Neckar, or explored the fog surrounding the Schloss. I remember the taste of cauliflower soup at the pub we ate dinner in, and the sour candy we frequently purchased for dessert at the musty candy store across the street, ran by an elderly man with a shaved head we were convinced was a war criminal in hiding.

And the beer! Ah, the beer. Delicious and thick, never ice-cold, with a head that forced me to be patient with each order in (Toph was right ... I did fall love with Dunkelbier). We drank Henniger often, because it was cheap, and close to Moorhaus, and it was good by American standards. But several times we would treat ourselves to a pint of Lowenbrau, dark. This bier was so rich that we consumed it delicately, purposefully, savoring each mouthful with appropriate thankfulness.

On the way back up the hill, there was a Jewish cemetery. Most of the Jewish cemeteries in Germany had been destroyed, and this one, for some reason, had been spared. I climbed the wall one day and sat on a bench for a long afternoon, bundled well, and soaked in the quiet, and the sadness. I remember not knowing why I was there or what I was looking for. It was one of many places I went with journal in hand, yet had no words to save. This, like many other experiences, was a part of my leapfrog journey to faith, a stumbling toward the light by means of the mystic, the mysterious, and even the mournful.

As I'm sitting here, I'm wondering what I'm yearning for. Why have I become so instantly nostalgic, so longing for youth, so longing for Heidelberg? I don't know. Perhaps a boredom with this suburbia, with the whole concept of adulthood (bills to pay of course ... but there's a dream on the tip of my tongue). A well-manicured lawn will never satisfy the heaving in my breast. I am amazed at how well my mind can recall feelings, excitements, longings. Vivid imagery. This leads me to believe that my time there was heightened. Dreamlike, and yet wonderfully alive. It was my first brush with living history, a land thick with culture and beauty. It was there I first realized that passion for life, and praise for the Giver of life, were one and the same. Perhaps the philosophy of appreciation isn't hopelessly far off after all.

In my travels since, in my search for life and newness, I am realizing that in all sorts of questing behaviors, I am seeking to return to the freedom, and the beauty, of Heidelberg in my twentieth year. It was there my heart began to seek God, and it was there I sensed, for the first time perhaps, that God was seeking me. Ultimately, those who seek, find.

Conclusion: Seek. Seek life. Seek HIM. Seek your deep desires. Seek your rollicking passions. And when you plumb the depths

of you, when you move through the shallow and the greedy and
the hedonistic and the cultural, when you get to the roots and the
deep soil of soul, you'll find that fulfillment is not an answer, but an
Answerer. When you shake free of the clammy hands of the pop-you,
the relevant-you, the you-as-your-own-ultimate-concern, and you go
to a more foundational human place, you will find what every mystic
through the ages has found: that Life itself is a pilgrimage to glory. It's
time to get swept off your feet.

You'll find, as I found in Heidelberg, that though you may begin to
seek God, He has been seeking you all along.

"Under the spell of this fairy-tale
The wanderers stand still.
Move on who can!
Perhaps they have seen it thus in dreams
And to each it seems like hearth and home,
And its magic look has never yet deceived,
For it is Heidelberg where they have now arrived"
—EICHENDORFF

"If I were called upon to state in a few words the essence of
everything I was trying to say, both as a novelist and as a preacher,
it would be something like this: listen to your life. See it for the
fathomless mystery that it is. In the boredom and pain of it no less
than in the excitement and gladness; touch, taste, smell your way
to the holy and hidden heart of it because in the last analysis, all
moments are key moments and life itself is grace."
—FREDERICK BUECHNER

172

A PILGRIM'S PRAYER

Thus says the Lord:
"Stand by the roads, and look, and ask for the ancient paths, where the good way is; and walk in it, and find rest for your souls." —Jeremiah 6:16

Life is good, friend; God is better. His is the Ancient Path, the most ancient of all paths. His is the Good Way. His is the Way of Rest. His contains the deep longings of your soul. In this verse, however, some choices are laid bare. God's blessing comes on the other side of decision. Only you can make that decision.

Ask for it, He says.

Walk in it, He urges.

Those are the choices. My prayer is that you would choose wisely. I'm a living testimony that wherever you wander, no matter how you roam, you do so under the eye of a loving God, who loves the pilgrim, the sinner, and the saint ... which is good news, because that's who I am. You too. You can trust His heart for you.

My daughter Alex is three, my son Caleb is one, and there are times when they reveal the very heart of God. Last year, my wife Jodie and

MILES TO CROSS

I were on our way to another church event, and we were gathering kids and diaper bags and going in different directions quickly. Jodie was taking care of the boy, and I was strapping my girl into her car-seat while coaching fast instructions to the babysitter who was in the driver's seat, but the greater part of my mind was thinking about the responsibilities I had ahead of me that evening. In the midst of that storm, I felt a tiny hand brush my cheek. It was so unexpected that I stopped talking. I stopped moving. I felt my daughter's tiny hand stroke my cheek again. Because I had stopped talking and because I had stopped moving, I could also hear that she was whispering in her solemn, clear-eyed way. So I carefully leaned in to hear what she was saying. "Beautiful." She said. "So beautiful. Daddy's so beautiful. So beautiful."

My encouragement as you travel your road is that you will stop talking long enough, and stop moving long enough to feel God's hand brush your cheek. My prayer is that you will lean in close and listen to His gentle, present, empowering whisper as He declares you, "Beautiful. So beautiful. You are so beautiful."

Because you are.

There's still time to change the road you're on.

May the Lord of the Road guide yours.

Amen.

ABOUT THE AUTHOR

Mike Howerton loves wrestling on the floor with his kids, reading Tolkien, surfing, and traveling to Italy (this mostly in his mind while listening to Van Morrison). He's been working for God for the last twelve years, always focused on the under-twenty-four population. Mike develops College Ministry Resources (www.craveresources.com) and loves watching God move in this generation. He currently serves at Saddleback Church, as the College Pastor, where he spends his time loving on people who are far hipper and smarter than he is. He lives in the OC with ultra-cool wife Jodie, angel-sweet daughter Alex, and roaring-bear-cub son Caleb.